Cádiz &
Costa de
la Luz

Andy Symington

Credits

Footprint credits
Editor: Jo Williams
Production and layout: Emma Bryers
Maps: Kevin Feeney

Managing Director: Andy Riddle
Content Director: Patrick Dawson
Publisher: Alan Murphy
Publishing Managers: Felicity Laughton,
Jo Williams, Nicola Gibbs
Marketing and Partnerships Director:
Liz Harper
Marketing Executive: Liz Eyles
Trade Product Manager: Diane McEntee
Account Managers: Paul Bew, Tania Ross
Advertising: Renu Sibal, Elizabeth Taylor
Finance: Phil Walsh

Photography credits
Front cover: Alon Boidek/Dreamstime
Back cover: Stewie74/Dreamstime

Printed in Great Britain by 4edge Limited,
Hockley, Essex

Every effort has been made to ensure that
the facts in this guidebook are accurate.
However, travellers should still obtain advice
from consulates, airlines, etc, about travel
and visa requirements before travelling.
The authors and publishers cannot accept
responsibility for any loss, injury or
inconvenience however caused.

Publishing information
Footprint *Focus Cádiz & Costa de la Luz*
1st edition
© Footprint Handbooks Ltd
April 2012

ISBN: 978 1 908206 59 6
CIP DATA: A catalogue record for this book
is available from the British Library

® Footprint Handbooks and the Footprint
mark are a registered trademark of
Footprint Handbooks Ltd

Published by Footprint
6 Riverside Court
Lower Bristol Road
Bath BA2 3DZ, UK
T +44 (0)1225 469141
F +44 (0)1225 469461
footprinttravelguides.com

Distributed in the USA by Globe Pequot
Press, Guilford, Connecticut

The content of Footprint *Focus Cádiz &
Costa de la Luz* has been taken directly from
Footprint's *Andalucía Handbook* which was
researched and written by Andy Symington.

Contents

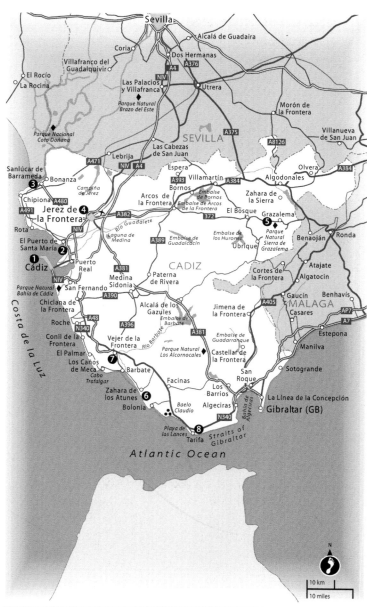

Of all Spain's provinces, Cádiz perhaps offers the greatest variety for a visitor; it has everything, whether you're a wine buff, windsurfer, seafood fanatic, horse fancier, architecture *aficionado*, beachcomber or notorious night owl.

Blessed with an Atlantic coastline, Cádiz attracts those who love long, sandy beaches with no golf hotels or all-day English breakfasts. The very wind that has kept development to a minimum is what makes the Costa de la Luz a favourite for wind- and kitesurfers. Clear views of the Moroccan coast add a spicy African feel to relaxed places like Tarifa, while curious Gibraltar, one of the ancients' Pillars of Hercules, marks the entrance to the Mediterranean.

Cádiz itself appeals for its setting on a promontory, its maze of narrow streets, a fabulous beach and wonderfully irreverent inhabitants. The city that celebrates Spain's most cutting-edge Carnaval still carries whispers of its past maritime greatness; it also has a cracking nightlife. Its larger counterpart, Jerez de la Frontera, is a complete contrast: a staid, dignified place, centre of the wealthy sherry trade and the famed Carthusian horses. There's more sherry in the towns west of Jerez: the favoured summering spots of El Puerto de Santa María and Sanlúcar de Barrameda. Sanlúcar's dry sherry, known as *manzanilla*, is the perfect accompaniment to seafood, in itself a revelation.

The province's hilly interior is speckled with whitewashed villages; many conserve their original Moorish street plan. As long as you don't go when it rains, the hills and mountains around Grazalema offer some of Andalucía's best and most varied walking.

Planning your trip

Best time to visit Cádiz and Costa de la Luz

Andalucía has one of mainland Europe's most agreeable climates. Winters are mild with some rain, but plenty of sunshine; coastal temperatures in January average 15-17°C. It is colder inland, particularly in the mountains.

Summers are hot, especially inland, but the coast benefits from pleasant seabreezes, particularly along the stretch from Gibraltar to Cádiz, where the strong *levante* wind can last for days on end, much to the joy of windsurfers. In summer, it can seem like most of Spain and half of Europe are lined up along Andalucía's beaches. While the atmosphere is good, the crowding and overpriced accommodation might induce you to pick the June or September shoulder season, when there's still plenty of sun. In high summer, inland temperatures soar.

Spring and autumn, are ideal seasons to visit Andalucía. Spring is the best time for birdwatching and wildflowers, temperatures are warm but not extreme, and there are many important festivals. Easter week itself is a major holiday in Spain and accommodation prices are very high. In autumn, the sea is still pleasantly warm and hiking conditions in the hills are at their best.

Cádiz's Carnaval in February or March is an unforgettable experience (see box, page 31), but you'll have to book accommodation well ahead. The city is at its liveliest in summer, when the beaches are packed day and night.

Getting to Cádiz and Costa de la Luz

Air
The growth of the budget sector means that there are now numerous options for reaching Andalucía. Five airports in the region (Sevilla, Málaga, Almería, and Jerez de la Frontera, as well as Gibraltar) are served regularly by flights from a wide variety of European cities; add in all the standard and charter flights, and it's one of Europe's easiest destinations to reach.

Charter flights are cheaper and are run by package holiday firms. You can find bargains through travel agencies or online. The drawback of these flights is that they usually have a fixed return flight, often no more than four weeks, and they frequently depart at antisocial hours. An upside is that charter flights operate from many regional airports.

Before booking, it's worth doing a bit of online research. Two of the best search engines for flight comparisons are www.opodo.com and www.kayak.com, which compare prices from a range of agencies. To keep yourself up to date with the ever-changing routes of the bewildering number of budget airlines, www.whichbudget.com is handy. Flightchecker (http://flightchecker.moneysavingexpert.com) is handy for checking multiple dates for budget airline deals.

Flights from the UK Competition has benefited travellers in recent years. Budget operators have taken a significant slice of the market and forced other airlines to compete.

Budget: There are numerous budget connections from the UK to Málaga. Easyjet and Ryanair connect Málaga with over a dozen UK airports, while other budget airlines running various routes from the UK to Málaga include Flybe, Aer Lingus, Norwegian, BMIBaby, Jet2, and Monarch. Sevilla is served by **Ryanair** from London, East Midlands, Liverpool and

Don't miss...

Bristol, and by **Vueling** and **Easyjet** from London Gatwick. Ryanair also flies to Jerez de la Frontera from Stansted. **Monarch** flies to Gibraltar from London Luton and Manchester, while Easyjet flies there from Gatwick and Liverpool.

Charter: There are numerous charter flights to Málaga (and some to Almería) from many British and Irish airports. **Avro** (www.avro.co.uk) and **First Choice** (www.firstchoice. co.uk) are a couple of the best charter flight providers, but it's also worth checking the travel pages of newspapers for cheap deals. The website www.flightsdirect.com is also a good tool to search for charter flights.

Non-budget flights: Málaga again has the most scheduled flights, with several airlines including **Iberia** and **British Airways** flying direct from London airports. There are daily direct flights to Sevilla with Iberia from London Heathrow and Gatwick, as well as numerous opportunities for connections via Madrid and Barcelona.

Flights from the rest of Europe There are numerous budget airlines operating from European and Spanish cities to Málaga. The website www.whichbudget.com is an essential tool to keep track of these services, as the market changes frequently.

Numerous charter flights operate to Málaga from Germany, Scandinavia, France, the Netherlands and Belgium.

There are non-stop flights to Málaga with non-budget airlines from many major European cities. There are daily non-stop flights to Sevilla from Paris and Brussels. Flying from these or other western European cities via Madrid or Barcelona usually costs about the same.

Flights from North America and Canada There are fortnightly charter flights from Montreal and Toronto with **Air Transat**. Otherwise, you'll have to connect via Madrid, Barcelona, London or another European city to Andalucían airports. Although some airlines throw in a free connecting flight to Málaga or Sevilla, you can usually save considerably by flying to Madrid and getting the bus down south (or book a domestic connection on the local no-frills airline **Vueling**, www.vueling.com).

Flights from Australia and New Zealand There are no direct flights to Spain from Australia or New Zealand; the cheapest and quickest way is to connect via Frankfurt, Paris or London. It might turn out cheaper to book the Europe–Spain leg separately via a budget operator.

Rail

Unless you've got a railpass or you aren't too keen on planes, forget about getting to Andalucía by train from anywhere further than France; you'll save no money over the plane fare and use up days of time better spent in tapas bars. You'll have to connect via either Barcelona or Madrid. Getting to Madrid/Barcelona from London takes about a day using **Eurostar** ① *www.eurostar.com, £75-200 return to Paris, and another €130 or more return to reach Madrid/Barcelona from there*. Using the ferry across the Channel adds eight or more hours and saves up to £100.

If you are planning the train journey, **Rail Europe** ① *T0844-484064, www.raileurope. co.uk*, is a useful company. **RENFE**, Spain's rail network, has online timetables at www. renfe.com. Also see the extremely useful www.seat61.com.

Road

Car and ferry It's a long haul to Andalucía by road if you're not already in the peninsula. From the UK, you have two options if you want to take the car: take a ferry to northern Spain (www.brittany-ferries.co.uk), or cross the Channel to France and then drive down. The former option is much more expensive; it would usually work out far cheaper to fly to Andalucía and hire a car once you get there. For competitive fares by sea to France and Spain, check with **Ferrysavers** ① *T0844-576 8835, www.ferrysavers.com*.

Andalucía is about 2000 km from London by road; a dedicated drive will get you there in 20-24 driving hours. By far the fastest route is to head down the west coast of France, to Madrid via San Sebastián then south towards Jaén and Córdoba.

Bus The advent of budget airlines has effectively removed the tiring and overpriced international bus routes from the equation when deciding on how to get to southern Spain. **Eurolines** ① *T01582-404511, www.eurolines.com*, runs several buses from major European cities to a variety of destinations in Andalucía.

Transport in Cádiz and Costa de la Luz

Air

Andalucía has several airports that are serviced regularly from Barcelona and Madrid, but there are no flights between the cities themselves, so once you're in the region, you're better off staying on the ground rather than backtracking through Madrid. Full-fare domestic flights are expensive, but budget airlines **Vueling**, **Easyjet** and **Ryanair** all offer domestic routes. Most internal flights in Spain are operated by **Iberia**; **Spanair** and **Air Europa** also run some routes. If you're flying into Spain from overseas, a domestic leg can often be added at comparatively little cost.

If you're flying into Spain from outside Europe on a **OneWorld** affiliate airline, you may want to consider the OneWorld Visit Europe airpass, which offers set-rate flights with Iberia that cost €55 for up to 318 km, or €80 up to 638 km. The same rates apply for flights all around Europe. See www.oneworld.com for more details.

Rail

The Spanish national rail network, **RENFE** ① *T902-240202 (English-speaking operators), www.renfe.es for timetables and tickets*, is, thanks to its growing network of high-speed trains, a useful option. **AVE** trains run from Madrid to Córdoba, Sevilla and Málaga and, though expensive, cover these large distances impressively quickly and reliably. Elsewhere in Andalucía though, you'll find the bus is often quicker and cheaper.

Prices vary significantly according to the type of service you are using. The standard high-speed intercity service is called *Talgo*, while other intercity services are labelled *Altaria*, *Intercity*, *Diurno* and *Estrella* (overnight). Slower local trains are called *regionales*. Alvia is a mixed AVE-Talgo service.

It's always worth buying a ticket in advance for long-distance travel, as trains are often full. The best option is to buy them via the website, which sometimes offers advance purchase discounts. You can also book by phone, but only Spanish cards are accepted. In either case, you get a reservation code, then print off your ticket at the terminals at the station. If buying your ticket at the station, allow plenty of time for queuing. Ticket windows are labelled *venta anticipada* (in advance) and *venta inmediata* (six hours or less before the journey). A better option can be to use a travel agent; the ones in town that sell tickets will display a RENFE sign, but you'll have to buy them a day in advance. Commission is minimal.

All Spanish trains are non-smoking. The faster trains will have a first-class (*preferente*) and second-class sections as well as a *cafetería*. First class costs about 30% more than standard and can be a worthwhile deal on a crowded long journey. Other pricing is bewilderingly complex. Night trains are more expensive, even if you don't take a sleeping berth, and there's a system of peak/off-peak days that makes little difference in practice. Buying a return ticket is 10% to 20% cheaper than two singles, but you qualify for this discount even if you buy the return leg later (but not on every service).

An **ISIC student card** or **under-26 card** grants a discount of 20% to 25% on train services. If you're using a European railpass, be aware that you'll still have to make a reservation on Spanish trains and pay the small reservation fee (which covers your insurance). If you have turned 60, it's worth paying €5 for a Tarjeta Dorada, a seniors' card that gets you a discount of 40% on trains from Monday to Thursday, and 25% at other times.

Road

Buses are the staple of Spanish public transport. Services between major cities are fast, frequent, reliable and fairly cheap; the six-hour trip from Madrid to Sevilla, for example, costs €20. When buying a ticket, always check how long the journey will take, as the odd bus will be an 'all stations to' job, calling in at villages that seem surprised to even see it.

While some cities have several departure points for buses, most have a single terminal, the *estación de autobuses*. Buy your tickets at the relevant window; if there isn't one, buy it from the driver. Most tickets will have an *asiento* (seat number) on them; ask when buying the ticket if you prefer a *ventana* (window) or *pasillo* (aisle) seat. Some of the companies allow booking online or by phone; the website www.movelia.es is the most useful. If you're travelling at busy times (particularly a fiesta or national holiday) always book the bus ticket in advance.

Rural bus services are slower, less frequent and more difficult to coordinate.

All bus services are reduced on Sundays and, to a lesser extent, on Saturdays; some services don't run at all on weekends. Local newspapers publish a comprehensive list of departures.

Car The roads in Andalucía are good, excellent in many parts. While driving isn't as sedate as in parts of northern Europe, it's generally pretty good and you'll have few problems. The roads near the coast, dense with partygoers and sunseekers, can be dangerous in summer, particularly the stretch along the Costa del Sol.

To drive in Spain, you'll need a full driving licence from your home country. This applies to virtually all foreign nationals but, in practice, if you're from an 'unusual' country, consider an International Driving Licence or official translation of your licence into Spanish.

There are two types of motorway in Spain, *autovías* and *autopistas*; for drivers, they are little different. They are signposted in blue and may have tolls payable, in which case there'll be a red warning circle on the blue sign when you're entering the motorway. Tolls are generally reasonable; the quality of motorway is generally excellent. The speed limit on motorways is 120 kph.

Rutas Nacionales form the backbone of the country's road network. Centrally administered, they vary wildly in quality. Typically, they are choked with traffic backed up behind trucks, and there are few stretches of dual carriageway. Driving at siesta time is a good idea if you're going to be on a busy stretch. *Rutas Nacionales* are marked with a red N followed by a number. The speed limit is 100 kph outside built-up areas, as it is for secondary roads, which are usually marked with an A (Andalucía), or C (*comarcal*, or local) prefix.

In urban areas, the speed limit is 50 kph. City driving can be confusing, with signposting generally poor and traffic heavy; it's worth printing off the directions that your hotel may send you with a reservation. In some towns and cities, many of the hotels are officially signposted, making things easier. Larger cities may have their historic quarter blocked off by barriers; if your hotel lies within these, ring the buzzer and say the name of the hotel, and the barriers will open. Other cities enforce restrictions by camera, so you'll have to give your number plate details to the hotel so they can register it.

Police are increasingly enforcing speed limits in Spain, and foreign drivers are liable to a large on-the-spot fine. Drivers can also be punished for not carrying two red warning triangles to place on the road in case of breakdown, a bulb-replacement kit and a fluorescent green waistcoat to wear if you break down by the side of the road. Drink driving is being cracked down on; the limit is 0.5 g/l of blood, slightly less than the equivalent in the UK, for example.

Parking is a problem in nearly every town and city in Andalucía. Red or yellow lines on the side of the street mean no parking. Blue or white lines mean that some restrictions are in place; a sign will indicate what these are (typically it means that the parking is metered). Parking meters can usually only be dosed up for a maximum of two hours, but they take a siesta at lunchtime too. Print the ticket off and display it in the car. If you overstay and get fined, you can pay it off for minimal cost at the machine if you do it within an hour of the fine being issued. Parking fines are never pursued for foreign vehicles, but if it's a hire car you'll possibly be liable for it. Underground car parks are common, but pricey; €15-20 a day is normal.

Liability insurance is required for every car driven in Spain and you must carry proof of it. If bringing your own car, check carefully with your insurers that you're covered and get a certificate (green card).

Hiring a car in Andalucía is easy and relatively cheap. The major multinationals have offices at all large towns and airports. Prices start at around €150 per week for a small car with unlimited mileage. You'll need a credit card and most agencies will either not accept under-25s or demand a surcharge. By far the cheapest place to hire a car is Málaga, where even at the airport there are competitive rates. With the bigger companies, it's always cheaper to book over the internet. The best way to look for a deal is using a price-comparison website like www.kelkoo.com or www.kayak.com.

Cycling and motorcycling Motorcycling is a good way to enjoy Andalucía and there are few difficulties to trouble the biker; bike shops and mechanics are relatively common. There are comparatively few outlets for motorcycle hire.

Cycling presents a curious contrast; Spaniards are mad for the competitive sport, but essentially disinterested in cycling as a means of transport, though local governments are trying to encourage it with new bike lanes and free borrowable bikes in places like Sevilla. Thus there are plenty of cycling shops but few cycle-friendly features on the roads. Taking your own bike to Andalucía is well worth the effort as most airlines are happy to accept them, providing they come within your baggage allowance. Bikes can be taken on the train, but have to travel in the guard's van and must be registered.

Hitchhiking Hitchhiking is fairly easy in Spain, although not much practised. The police aren't too keen on it, but with sensible placement and a clearly written sign, you'll usually get a lift without a problem, particularly in rural areas, where, in the absence of bus services, it's a more common way for locals to get about.

Taxi and bus Most Andalucían cities have their sights closely packed into the centre, so you won't find local buses particularly necessary. There's a fairly comprehensive network in most towns, though; the travel text indicates where they come in handy. Taxis are a good option; the minimum charge is around €2.50 in most places (it increases slightly at night and on Sundays). A taxi is available if its green light is lit; hail one on the street, call, or ask for the nearest *parada de taxis* (rank). If you're using a cab to get to somewhere beyond the city limits, there are fixed tariffs.

Maps
A useful website for route planning is www.guiarepsol.com. Car hire companies have navigation systems available, though they cost a hefty supplement.

Where to stay in Cádiz and Costa de la Luz

The standard of accommodation in Andalucía is very high; even the most modest of *pensiones* is usually very clean and respectable. *Alojamientos* (places to stay), are divided into two main categories; the distinctions between them are in an arcane series of regulations devised by the government. *Hoteles* (marked H or HR) are graded from one to five stars and occupy their own building, which distinguishes them from many *hostales* (Hs or HsR), which go from one to two stars. The *hostal* category includes *pensiones*, the standard budget option, typically family-run and occupying a floor of an apartment building. The standard for the price paid is normally excellent, and they're nearly all spotless. Spanish traditions of hospitality are alive and well; even the simplest of *pensiones* will generally provide a towel and soap, and check-out time is almost uniformly a very civilized midday.

A great number of Spanish hotels are well equipped but characterless chain business places (big players include **NH**, www.nh-hoteles.es; **Husa**, www.husa.es; **AC**, www.ac-hotels.com; **Tryp/SolMelia**, www.solmelia.com and **Hesperia**, www.hoteles-hesperia.es), and are often situated outside the old town. This guide has expressly minimized these in the listings, preferring to concentrate on more atmospheric options. If you're booking accommodation not listed in this guide, always be sure to check the location if that's important to you – it's easy to find yourself a 15-minute cab ride from the town you think you're going to be in.

Price codes

Where to stay

€€€€ over €170   €€€ €110-170
€€ €55-110   € under €55

Price codes refer to the cost of a standard double/twin room in high season.

Restaurants

€€€ over €30   €€ €15-30   € under €15

Price codes refer to the cost of a two-course meal (or two average *raciones*) for one person, excluding drinks.

An excellent option if you've got your own transport are the networks of rural houses, called *casas rurales*. Although these are under a different classification system, the standard is often as high as any country hotel. The best of them are traditional farmhouses or characterful village cottages. Some are available only to rent out whole (often for a minimum of three days), while others offer rooms on a nightly basis. Rates tend to be excellent compared to hotels. While many are listed in the text, there are huge numbers of them. Local tourist offices will have details of nearby *casas rurales*; there's also a complete listing for Andalucía available, although it's often out of stock. You can buy the useful *Guía de Alojamiento Rural*, published by El País/Aguilar, from most bookshops. Another excellent resource for finding and booking rural accommodation is the website www.toprural.com, though the star ratings given by users tend to be overinflated.

There's a network of *albergues* (youth hostels), which are listed at www.inturjoven. com. These are all open year round and are very comfortable, though institutional and not especially cheap.

Most campsites are set up as well-equipped holiday villages for families; some are open only in summer. While the facilities are good, they get extremely busy in peak season; the social scene is lively, but sleep can be tough. Many have cabins or bungalows available, ranging from simple huts to houses with fully equipped kitchens and bathrooms. In other areas, camping, unless specifically prohibited, is a matter of common sense.

All registered accommodations charge a 8% value added tax; this is often included in the price at cheaper places and may be waived if you pay cash (tut tut). If you have any problems, a last resort is to ask for the *libro de reclamaciones* (complaints book), an official document that, like stepping on cracks in the pavement, means uncertain but definitely horrible consequences for the hotel if anything is written in it. If resorting to this, be aware that you must also take a copy to the local police station for the complaint to be registered.

Price codes refer to a standard double or twin room, inclusive of VAT. The rates are generally for high season. Occasionally, an area or town will have a short period when prices are hugely exaggerated; this is usually due to a festival such as Cádiz's Carnaval. Low-season accommodation can be significantly cheaper; up to half in some coastal areas.

Many mid- to top-range city hotels cater for business travellers during the week and keep prices accordingly high. The flipside is that they usually have special weekend rates that can be exceptionally good value. Typically, these involve staying on the Friday and Saturday night and prebooking. Breakfast will often be thrown in *gratis* and the whole deal can save you more than 50% on the quoted prices. It's always worth investigating these and other offers by phoning ahead or checking the website.

The most useful websites for saving on hotel rates in Spain are www.booking.com, www.hotels.com and www.laterooms.com.

Normally only the more expensive hotels have parking, and they always charge for it, normally around €10-18 per day. Breakfast is often included in the price at small intimate hotels, but rarely at the grander places, who tend to charge a fortune for what is nothing more than bog-standard morning fare. Similarly, chain hotels tend to charge exorbitant rates for things like Wi-Fi, which are usually free at humbler places.

Food and drink in Cádiz and Costa de la Luz

In no country in the world are culture and society as intimately connected with eating and drinking as in Spain, and in Andalucía, the spiritual home of tapas, this is even more the case. Spain's food and drink culture is significantly different from elsewhere in the EU.

Food

Andalucían cooking is characterized by an abundance of fresh ingredients, generally consecrated with the chef's holy trinity of garlic, peppers and, of course, local olive oil.

Spaniards eat little for breakfast and, apart from in touristy places, you're unlikely to find anything beyond a *tostada* (large piece of toasted bread spread with olive oil, tomato and garlic, paté or jam) or a pastry to go with your coffee. Another common breakfast or afternoon snack are *churros*, long fried doughnuts that will either delight or disgust, and are typically dipped in cups of hot chocolate.

Lunch is most people's main meal of the day and is nearly always a filling affair with three courses. Most places open for lunch at about 1300, and stop serving food at 1500 or 1530, although at weekends this can extend. Lunchtime is the cheapest time to eat if you opt for the ubiquitous *menú del día*, usually a set three-course meal that includes wine or soft drink, typically costing €9 to €15. Dinner and/or evening tapas time is from around 2100 to midnight. It's not much fun sitting alone in a restaurant so try and adapt to the local hours; it may feel strange leaving dinner until so late, but you'll miss out on a lot of atmosphere if you don't. If a place is open for lunch at noon, or dinner at 1900, it's likely to be a tourist trap.

The great joy of eating out in Andalucía is, of course, going for tapas. This word refers to bar food, which is served in saucer-sized tapa portions typically costing €1.50-3. Tapas customs vary slightly from province to province. Tapas are available at lunchtime, but the classic time to eat them is in the evening. To do tapas the Andalucían way don't order more than a couple at each place, taste each others' dishes, and stay put at the bar. Locals know what the specialities of each bar are; it's worth asking, and if there's a daily special, order that. Also available are *raciones*, substantial meal-sized plates of the same fare, which also come in halves, *media raciones*. Both varieties are good for sharing. Considering these, the distinction between restaurants and tapas bars more or less disappears, as in the latter you can usually sit down at a table to order your *raciones*, effectively turning the experience into a meal.

Other types of eateries include the *chiringuito*, a beach bar open in summer and serving drinks and fresh seafood. A *freiduría* is a takeaway specializing in fried fish, while a *marisquería* is a classier type of seafood restaurant. In rural areas, look out for *ventas*, roadside eateries that often have a long history of feeding the passing muleteers with generous, hearty and cheap portions. The more cars and trucks outside, the better it will be.

Vegetarians in Andalucía won't be spoiled for choice, but at least what there is tends to be good. There are few dedicated vegetarian restaurants and many restaurants won't have a vegetarian main course on offer, although the existence of tapas, *raciones* and salads makes this less of a burden than it might be. You'll have to specify *soy vegetariano/a* (I am a vegetarian), but ask what dishes contain, as ham, fish and even chicken are often considered suitable vegetarian fare. Vegans will have a tougher time.

Typical starters you'll see on set menus include *gazpacho* (a cold summer tomato soup flavoured with garlic, olive oil and peppers; *salmorejo* is a thicker version from Córdoba), *ensalada mixta* (mixed salad based on lettuce, tomatoes, tuna and more), or paella.

Main courses will usually be either meat or fish and are almost never served with any accompaniment beyond chips or marinated peppers. Beef is common throughout; cheaper cuts predominate, but better steaks such as *solomillo* or *entrecot* are usually superbly tender. Spaniards tend to eat them rare (*poco hecho*; ask for *al punto* for medium rare or *bien hecho* for well done). Pork is also widespread; *solomillo de cerdo*, *secreto*, *pluma* and *lomo* are all tasty cuts. Animal innards are popular: *callos* (tripe), *mollejas* (sweetbreads) and *morcilla* (black pudding) are excellent, if acquired, tastes.

Seafood is the pride of Andalucía. The region is famous for its *pescaíto frito* (fried fish) which typically consists of small fry such as whitebait in batter. Shellfish include *mejillones* (mussels), *gambas* (prawns) and *coquillas* (cockles). *Calamares* (calamari), *sepia* or *choco* (cuttlefish) and *chipirones* (small squid) are common, and you'll sometimes see *pulpo* (octopus). Among the vertebrates, *sardinas* (sardines), *dorada* (gilthead bream), *rape* (monkfish) and *pez espada* (swordfish) are all usually excellent.

Signature tapas dishes vary from bar to bar and from province to province, and part of the delight of Andalucía comes trying regional specialities. Ubiquitous are *jamón* (cured ham; the best, *ibérico*, comes from black-footed acorn-eating porkers that roam the woods of Huelva province and Extremadura) and *queso* (usually the hard salty *manchego* from Castilla-la Mancha). *Gambas* (prawns) are usually on the tapas list; the best and priciest are from Huelva. *Adobe* is marinated fried nuggets of fish, usually dogfish.

Desserts focus on the sweet and milky. *Flan* (a sort of crème caramel) is ubiquitous; great when *casero* (homemade), but often out of a plastic tub. *Natillas* are a similar but more liquid version, while Moorish-style pastries are also specialities of some areas.

Drink

Alcoholic drinks In good Catholic fashion, wine is the blood of Spain. It's the standard accompaniment to most meals, but also features prominently in bars. *Tinto* is red (if you just order *vino* it's assumed that's what you want), *blanco* is white and rosé is *rosado*.

A well-regulated system of *denominaciones de origen* (DO), similar to the French *appelation controlée*, has lifted the quality and reputation of Spanish wines high above the party plonk status they once enjoyed. While the daddy in terms of production and popularity is still Rioja, regions such as the Ribera del Duero, Rueda, Bierzo, Jumilla, Priorat and Valdepeñas have achieved worldwide recognition. The words *crianza*, *reserva* and *gran reserva* refer to the length of the ageing process.

One of the joys of Spain, though, is the rest of the wine. Order a *menú del día* at a cheap restaurant and you'll be unceremoniously served a cheap bottle of local red. Wine snobbery can leave by the back door at this point: it may be cold, but you'll find it refreshing; it may be acidic, but once the olive-oil laden food arrives, you'll be glad of it. People add water to it if they feel like it, or *gaseosa* (lemonade) or cola (for the party drink *calimocho*).

Andalucía produces several table wines of this sort. The whites of the Condado region in eastern Huelva province and those from nearby Cádiz are simple seafood companions, while in the Alpujarra region the nut-brown *costa* is between a conventional red and a rosé. In the same area, Laujar de Andarax produces some tasty cheapish reds. Jaén province also has red grapes tucked between its seas of olive trees, mainly around Torreperogil near Úbeda. Bartenders throughout Andalucía tend to assume that tourists only want Rioja, so be sure to specify *vino corriente* (or *vino de la zona*) if you want to try the local stuff. As a general rule, only bars that serve food serve wine; most *pubs* and *discotecas* won't have it. Cheaper red wine is often served cold, a refreshing alternative in summer. Variations on the theme are *tinto de verano* (a summery mix of red wine and lemonade, often with fruit added) or the stronger *sangría*, which adds healthy measures of sherry and sometimes spirits to the mix. The real vinous fame of the region comes, of course, from its fortified wines; sherries and others (see box, page 43).

Beer is mostly lager, usually reasonably strong, fairly gassy, cold and good. Sweetish Cruzcampo from Sevilla is found throughout the region; other local brews include San Miguel, named after the archangel and brewed in Málaga, and Alhambra from Granada. A *caña* or *tubo* is a glass of draught beer, while just specifying *cerveza* usually gets you a bottle, otherwise known as a *botellín*. Many people order their beer *con gas*, topped up with mineral water, or order a *clara*, which is a shandy. A *jarra* is a shared jug. In some pubs, particularly those specializing in different beers, you can order *pintas* (pints).

Vermut (vermouth) is a popular pre-lunch aperitif. Many bars make their own vermouth by adding various herbs and fruits and letting it sit in barrels: this can be excellent, particularly if it's from a *solera* (see box, page 43).

After dinner it's time for a *copa*. People relax over a whisky or a brandy, or hit the *cubatas* (mixed drinks): *gin tonic* is obvious; whisky or rum with coke are the other mainstays. Spirits are free-poured and large.

When ordering a spirit, you'll be expected to choose which brand you want; the local varieties (eg Larios gin, DYC whisky) are marginally cheaper than their imported brethren but lower in quality. *Chupitos* are short drinks often served in shot-glasses; restaurants will often throw in a free digestive one (usually a herb liqueur) at the end of a meal.

Non-alcoholic drinks *Zumo* (fruit juice) is normally bottled and expensive; *mosto* (grape juice, really pre-fermented wine) is a cheaper and popular soft drink in bars. All bars serve alcohol-free beer (*cerveza sin alcohol*). *Horchata* is a summer drink, a sort of milkshake made from tiger nuts. *Agua* (water) comes *con* (with) or *sin* (without) *gas*. The tap water is totally safe to drink.

Café (coffee) is usually excellent and strong. *Solo* is black, mostly served espresso style. Order *americano* if you want a long black, *cortado* if you want a dash of milk, or *con leche* for about half milk. A *carajillo* is a coffee with brandy. *Té* (tea) is served without milk unless you ask; *infusiones* (herbal teas) can be found in most places.

Essentials A-Z

Accident and emergency
General emergencies 112 (the most reliable nationwide emergency number). Ambulance 061. Fire 080. Police 092.

Electricity
220V. A round 2-pin plug is used (European standard).

Embassies and consulates
For all Spanish embassies and consulates abroad and for all foreign embassies and consulates in Andalucía, see http://embassy.goabroad.com.

Health
Medical facilities in Andalucía are very good. However, EU citizens should make sure they have the **European Health Insurance Card** (EHIC) to prove reciprocal rights to medical care. These are available free of charge in the UK from the Department of Health (www.dh.gov.uk) or post offices.

 Non-EU citizens should consider travel insurance to cover emergency and routine medical needs; be sure that it covers any sports or activities you may do. Check for reciprocal cover with your private or public health scheme first.

 Water is safe to drink, but isn't always pleasant, so many travellers (and locals) stick to bottled water. The **sun** in southern Spain can be harsh, so take precautions to avoid heat exhaustion and sunburn.

 Many medications that require a prescription in other countries are available over the counter at pharmacies in Spain. Pharmacists are highly trained and usually speak some English. In medium-sized towns and cities, at least one pharmacy is open 24 hrs; this is performed on a rota system (posted in the window of all pharmacies and listed in local newspapers).

 No vaccinations are needed.

Language
Everyone in Andalucía speaks Spanish, known either as *castellano* or *español*, and it's a huge help to know some. The local accent, *andaluz*, is characterized by dropping consonants left, right and centre, thus *dos tapas* tends to be pronounced *dotapa*. Unlike in the rest of Spain, the letters 'c' and 'z' in words such as *cerveza* aren't pronounced 'th' (although in Cádiz province, perversely, they tend to pronounce 's' with that sound).

 Most young people know some English, and standards are rising, but don't assume that people aged 40 or over know any at all. Spaniards are often shy to attempt to speak English. On the coast, high numbers of expats and tourists mean that bartenders and shopkeepers know some English and to a lesser extent German and French. While many visitor attractions have some sort of information available in English (and to a lesser extent French and German), many don't, or have English tours only in times of high demand. Most tourist office staff will speak at least some English and there's a good range of translated information available in most places.

Language schools
Language schools are also listed within the main travel text in the Directory sections.
 Amerispan, PO Box 58129, 117 South 17th St, 14th Floor, Philadelphia, PA 19103, USA, T1-800-879 6640, www.amerispan.com. Immersion programmes throughout Spain.
 Languages Abroad, T01872-225 300, T1-800-219 9924 (USA/Can), www.languagesabroad.com. Immersion courses in Andalucían cities.
 Spanish Abroad, 5112 N 40th St, Suite 103, Phoenix AZ 85018, T1-602-778 6791, www.spanishabroad.com. 2-week immersion language courses in several Andalucían locations including Vejer de la Frontera.

Money

Currency and exchange

Exchange rates GBP1=€1.20, US$1=€0.75. (Mar 2012). For up-to-the-minute exchange rates visit www.xe.com.

In 2002, Spain switched to the euro, bidding farewell to the peseta. The euro (€) is divided into 100 *céntimos*. Euro notes are standard across the whole zone and come in denominations of 5, 10, 20, 50, 100, and the rarely seen 200 and 500. Coins have one standard face and one national face; all coins are, however, acceptable in all countries. The coins are slightly difficult to tell apart when you're not used to them. The coppers are 1, 2 and 5 cent pieces, the golds are 10, 20 and 50, and the silver/gold combinations are €1 and €2. The exchange rate was approximately €6 to 1000 pesetas or 166 pesetas to the euro.

ATMs and banks

The best way to get money in Spain is by plastic. ATMs are plentiful and accept all the major international debit and credit cards. The Spanish bank won't charge for the transaction, though they will charge a mark-up on the exchange rate, but beware of your own bank hitting you for a hefty fee: check with them before leaving home. Even if they do, it's likely to be a better deal than changing cash over a counter.

Banks are usually open Mon-Fri (and Sat in winter) 0830-1400 and many change foreign money (sometimes only the central branch in a town will do it). Commission rates vary widely; it's usually best to change large amounts, as there's often a minimum commission. The website www.moneysavingexpert.com has a good rundown on the most economical ways of accessing cash while travelling.

Cost of living

Spain is much more expensive than it was, and for the traveller is no longer a money-saving destination. Nevertheless, it still offers value for money, and you can get by cheaply if you forgo a few luxuries. If you're travelling as a pair, staying in cheap *pensiones*, eating a set meal at lunchtime, travelling short distances by bus or train daily, and snacking on tapas in the evenings, €65 per person per day is reasonable. If you camp and grab picnic lunches from shops, you could reduce this somewhat. In a good *hostal* or cheap hotel and using a car, €150 a day and you'll not be counting pennies; €300 per day and you'll be very comfy indeed unless you're staying in 5-star accommodation.

Accommodation is usually more expensive in summer than winter, particularly on the coast, where hotels and *hostales* in seaside towns are overpriced. Accommodation over the major fiesta periods is very expensive; prices at Semana Santa can be double the norm. The news isn't great for the solo traveller; single rooms tend not to be particularly good value and they are in short supply. Prices range from 60% to 80% of the double/twin price; some establishments even charge the full rate. If you're going to be staying in 3- to 5-star hotels, booking them ahead on internet discount sites can save you money.

Public transport is generally cheap; intercity bus services are quick and low-priced, though the new fast trains are expensive. If you're hiring a car, Málaga is the cheapest place in Andalucía. Petrol costs have skyrocketed: standard unleaded petrol is around 138 cents per litre. In some places, particularly in tourist areas, you may be charged up to 20% more to sit outside a restaurant. It's also worth checking if the 8% IVA (sales tax) is included in menu prices, especially in the more expensive restaurants; it should say on the menu.

Opening hours

Business hours Mon-Fri 1000-1400, 1700-2000; Sat 1000-1400. **Banks** Mon-Fri, plus Sat in winter, 0830-1400. **Government offices** Mornings only.

Safety

Andalucía is a very safe place to travel. There's been a crackdown on tourist crime in recent years.

What tourist crime there is tends to be of the opportunistic kind. Robberies from parked cars (particularly those with foreign plates) or snatch-and-run thefts from vehicles stopped at traffic lights are not unknown. If parking in a city or a popular hiking zone, make it clear there's nothing worth robbing in a car by opening the glove compartment.

If you are unfortunate enough to be robbed, you should report the theft immediately at the nearest police station, as insurance companies will require a copy of the *denuncia* (police statement).

Tax

Nearly all goods and services in Spain are subject to a value-added tax (IVA). This is 8% for things like basic supermarket supplies, hotels and restaurant meals, but is 18% on luxury goods such as computer equipment. IVA is normally included in the stated prices. You're technically entitled to claim it back if you're a non-EU citizen, for purchases over €90. If you're buying something pricey, make sure you get a stamped receipt clearly showing the IVA component, as well as your name and passport number; you can claim the amount back at major airports on departure. Some shops will have a form to smooth the process.

Time

1 hr ahead of GMT.

Tipping

Tipping in Spain is far from compulsory. A 10% tip would be considered extremely generous in a restaurant; 3% to 5% is more usual. It's rare for a service charge to be added to a bill. Waiters don't expect tips for lunchtime set meals or tapas, but here and in bars and cafés people will often leave small change, especially for table service. Taxi drivers don't expect a tip, but will be pleased to receive one.

Visas and immigration

EU citizens and those from countries within the Schengen agreement can enter Spain freely. UK and Irish citizens will need to carry a passport, while an identity card suffices for other EU/Schengen nationals. Citizens of Australia, the USA, Canada, New Zealand and Israel can enter without a visa for up to 90 days. Other citizens will require a visa, obtainable from Spanish consulates or embassies. These are usually issued quickly and are valid for all Schengen countries. The basic visa is valid for 90 days, and you'll need 2 passport photos, proof of funds covering your stay, and possibly evidence of medical cover (ie insurance).

For extensions of visas, apply to an *oficina de extranjeros* in a major city (usually the *comisaría*, main police station).

Weights and measures

Metric.

Contents

Footprint features

Cádiz

Cádiz, one of Spain's most vibrant and lovable cities, was memorably described by Laurie Lee as "a scribble of white on a sheet of blue glass, lying curved on the bay like a scimitar and sparkling with African light". Its location is certainly spectacular, on a long narrow promontory with the Atlantic on one side and the Bahía de Cádiz on the other. The old town occupies the tip of the promontory; the extensive new town stretches several kilometres along the main town beach, Playa de la Victoria. This part of town is known as Puerta de Tierra, named after the city gates that give access to the old town.

With a proud and long maritime history stretching back to the Phoenicians, it comes as no surprise that Cádiz can seem less conservative and more outward looking than many Andalucían cities; geographically it's not far off being an island, and culturally it's typified by its riotous Carnaval.

Earthquakes and buccaneering have deprived it of monuments, but it's still a cracking place with the sea seemingly at the end of every narrow street. Watching the sunset from the beach or promenade is an experience to compare with any in Andalucía. The architecture of the old town is an elegant blend of 18th- and 19th-century houses, while beyond the old city gates stretches the interminable Avenida de Andalucía, running parallel to the town's long beaches with plenty of nightlife.

Arriving in Cádiz

Getting there
Cádiz has no airport, but is close to the international airport of Jerez de la Frontera, see page 52. The city is well connected by public transport, and is easily reached by bus or train from Sevilla or by bus from Málaga.

Getting around
Cádiz is forced by geography into being very long and thin. While the old town is reasonably compact, the new town is not. Bus No 1 runs every five minutes from the Plaza de España right down the length of the new town. You can also head to the new town by the *cercanía* train, which runs every 40 minutes or so, with several stops along the length of the beach. Segunda Aguada is the closest to the heart of the action. A journey in a cab from Plaza San Juan de Dios in the old town to the bars of the Paseo Marítimo should cost €5-7. There are plenty of ranks; otherwise T956-212121. ▶ *See Transport, page 32.*

Tourist information
The helpful Junta de Andalucía **tourist office** ① *C Nueva s/n, T956-258646, Mon-Fri 0900-1930, Sat and Sun 0930-1500,* is handily situated. At weekends, there's also a **kiosk** ① *Sat and Sun 1000-1330, 1600-1800 (1700-1900 summer),* open on Plaza San Juan de Dios and one on Avenida Carranza on the corner of Avenida de la Coruña near the football stadium a block back from the beach in the new town.

Background → *Phone code: 956. Population: 125,826.*

Cádiz has a claim to being Western Europe's oldest city. It was founded as Gadir by the Phoenicians, possibly as early as 1100 BC. Later classical sources claimed that the inhabitants of Tyre were told by an oracle to found a settlement beyond the Pillars of Hercules. The Phoenician name for the city lives on; today's inhabitants are called *gaditanos*. Archaeological discoveries indicate that ties to the Eastern Mediterranean remained strong even once Phoenician sea power had waned. The heirs and descendants of the Phoenicians, the Carthaginians, also established an important presence here. Caesar conferred full Roman citizenship on the *gaditanos* after the town helped him against Pompeii, but the city declined rapidly in the late Roman era and did not play a prominent part in the Moorish era. Cádiz began to benefit from the discovery of the Americas, and prospered greatly once the monopoly for Atlantic trade was moved here from Sevilla in the 18th century. The city's new status attracted the attention of foreign powers, who regularly looted the town.

During the Peninsular War, brave liberals invoked the ancient Spanish regional privileges and set up a parliament to rule in the absence of the king. These *cortes* drew up a constitution in 1812, which established a democratic parliamentary monarchy that became a blueprint for constitutional movements throughout Europe. The returning king, Fernando, revoked it, but it was re-proclaimed by a rebellious army colonel, Rafael de Riego, in 1820. Such was his support that the king admitted the legality of the 1812 document, but soon went back on his promise. In the wake of another advancing French army, the *cortes* fled back to Cádiz and surrendered in September 1823. Riego was executed. In the Civil War, Cádiz was firmly on the side of the left, but *Rusia chica* (little Russia), as it was known, couldn't hold out against the Nationalists. Franco banned Cádiz's exuberant Carnaval, but it survived by changing its name and date. Big celebrations are planned in Cádiz for the bicentenary of the constitution in 2012.

Places in Cádiz → *For listings, see pages 27-32.*

One of the charms of Cádiz is simply wandering around its maze of narrow streets; the attractive whitewashed houses typically have glassed-in balconies. Barrio del Pópulo, to the east of the cathedral, is one of the most traditional districts, as is Barrio de la Viña, the blocks behind Castillo de San Sebastián. One street here, Calle Pastora, is picturesquely festooned with flowerpots painted in the colours of the local football team. After a restoration programme these historic *barrios* are now looking spruce, without having lost their maritime character.

Cathedral
ⓘ *Plaza de la Catedral s/n, T956-286154. Mon-Sat 1000-1830, Sun 1330-1830, €5 including museum, free entry to cathedral only Sun 1100-1230.*
Especially picturesque when viewed from further around the waterfront, with its golden dome glinting, Cádiz's cathedral was built in the 18th and 19th centuries. Its main facade on Plaza de la Catedral is a blend of the late Baroque and the neoclassical and flanked by two graceful white towers. The interior is rather sombre and somewhat reminiscent of a Roman necropolis, with huge Corinthian columns looming in the shadows. A fine feature is the wonderful choir of cedar and mahogany, with carved figures of saints. The crypt below is a brilliantly realized space in sombre stone; the architectural precision is reflected by the astonishing echoes produced. Here is buried the *gaditano* composer Manuel de Falla.

Also worth looking out for are the elegant sacristy and a large monstrance used in the sober Corpus Christi processions. The effect of the high central dome is rather ruined by the netting that protects visitors from falling masonry.

Entry to the cathedral includes admission to its museum, tucked around the side on Plaza de Fray Félix. This is set in a charming building with an old columned patio that is more interesting than the artwork, particularly as an excavated Roman road runs through it. Of the paintings on display, a picture of the fierce Anglo-Dutch sacking of the town in 1596 stands out, as do two 16th-century works of the Judas Kiss and the Crowning of Thorns. Some massive 16th- to 19th-century pergamines sit in a large bookcase; in the same room is a letter from St Teresa to the Inquisitor-General sealed in an ivory reliquary. A collection of carved 17th- to 18th-century ivory crucifixes show fine craftsmanship.

One of the cathedral's towers, the **Torre de Poniente** ⓘ *T956-251788, daily 1000-1730 (1930 in summer), entry by guided tour every 30 mins, €4,* can be climbed as part of a guided tour. There are views over the Atlantic and along the coast.

Barrio del Pópulo
This was the heart of medieval Cádiz and is a small network of charming buildings and narrow streets that has tangibly benefited from recent refurbishment. On the Plaza de la Catedral, look out for the gateway with embrasures that marks the entrance to the district. Near the cathedral on the waterfront is a **Roman theatre** ⓘ *Mon and Wed-Sun 1000-1430, free,* dating to the first century BC, while on Calle San Juan de Dios is another of the gateways to the *barrio*, as well as a stretch of the old walls. The later walls, built after the attack of 1596, have mostly been taken down.

Tucked away behind the cathedral is the intriguing **Casa del Obispo** ⓘ *Plaza Fray Félix 5, T956-264734, daily 1000-1730 (1930 summer), €4.* The layers beneath this former bishop's residence have been peeled back to reveal remains of buildings from all of Cádiz's phases of occupation. It's an astonishing if sometimes confusing archaeological tour-de-force, exhibiting the foundations of Phoenician walls, fragments of Roman wall painting, part of what was possibly a Punic temple, and more. In one area once the episcopal stables, you can see the superimposition of one civilization upon the ruins of the last; it's contemplation of this, rather than struggling to understand individual stones, that makes the place fascinating.

At the edge of this *barrio*, the Plaza San Juan de Dios is dominated by the attractive **Ayuntamiento** (town hall), a typical example of neoclassical *gaditano* architecture. Nearby is a beautiful neo-Moorish former tobacco factory, dating from 1741. Further south is the main entrance to the city, the 18th-century **Puerta de Tierra** ① *Plaza de la Constitución s/n, T956-272709, daily 1000-1800, tower plus audiovisual or Sala Virtual €4, both €6*, which marks the boundary of the old and new towns. Though still an impressively muscular fortification, it was once much larger, offering the city complete protection from land assault. A visit starts with a 3D audiovisual show (English available) on the history of the city's defences; you then are guided to the top of the tower and given time to roam along the sturdy walls. The Sala Virtual offers a computer visit to the city's buildings as they would have been in their 18th-century maritime heyday.

Moving the other way from the cathedral, and following the waterfront, with rocks pounded by the Atlantic, you'll pass another historic *barrio* on your right, the **Barrio de la Viña**, before reaching the **Castillo de San Sebastián**. This fort is set on a small islet (joined to the mainland by a causeway in the 19th century) where some say the Phoenician temple of Melqart-Hercules once stood. It's a relaxing stroll out to the castle, now a lighthouse, but you can't enter the building itself.

Beyond is another castle, **Santa Catalina**, constructed after the British attacked. Built in a star shape to maximize firing arcs, it also has a small chapel. Between the two castles is **Playa de la Caleta** beach, backed by massive dragon trees. It's a legendary Cádiz spot, but in truth is not a remarkable beach.

Plaza de la Mina and around

In the north part of the old town, Plaza de la Mina is a large square near which are some of the city's best tapas bars. On the square itself is the excellent Museo de Cádiz (see below). On the south side of the square a plaque marks the house where the composer Manuel de Falla was born. Just east of here is another pleasant square, **Plaza San Francisco**, while to the south the larger **Plaza San Antonio** is dominated by its twin-towered Baroque church. North of Plaza de la Mina are the soothing waterside gardens, the **Alameda Marqués de Comillas**, which end at a defensive gun battery. East of the gardens, the large **Plaza de España** is marked by a monument to the Cádiz *cortes liberales*.

Museo de Cádiz

① *Plaza de la Mina s/n, T956-203368. Tue 1430-2030, Wed-Sat 0900-2030, Sun 0930-1430. Free for EU citizens, €1.50 for others.*

This excellent museum, one of the best in Andalucía, comprises both an archaeological and a fine arts section. The former, on the ground floor, is particularly notable for its **Phoenician** collection, with many finds from tombs in Cádiz and the surrounding area. There was an important temple of Melqart-Hercules here, as well as one of Astarte. In this section are some fine votive bronzes and terracotta busts, but the most striking objects are two huge anthropoid sarcophagi, one male, one female, carved from marble, and exhibiting strong stylistic influences from both Egypt and Greece. Found nearly a century

Cádiz

Bahía de Cádiz

Where to stay

Argantonio 2 *A4*
Casa Caracol 11 *B5*
Casa del Almirante 3 *C5*
Cuatro Naciones 7 *B5*
Hospedería Las Cortes
  de Cádiz 8 *A4*
Hostal Bahía 10 *B5*

Hostal Canalejas 9 *B5*
Hostal Fantoni 6 *B5*
Parador Atlántico 1 *B1*
Playa Victoria 19 *C6*
Regio 4 *C6*
Spa Cádiz Plaza 5 *C6*

Restaurants

Arte Serrano 10 *C6*
Bahía 18 *B5*
Casa Taberna
  Manteca 8 *C2*
Casa Tino 7 *C3*
El Balandro 3 *A3*
El Faro 6 *D2*

N

200 metres
200 yards

El Tendero **16** *B4*
Freiduría Las
  Flores **12** *B4, C6*
Gotinga **5** *B2*
Habana Café **24** *B4*
La Catedral **15** *C4*
La Gorda te da de
  Comer **9** *A4, B4*

Mesón Cumbres
  Mayores **13** *A3*
Puntaparilla **14** *C6*
Taberna San
  Francisco I **29** *A4*
Ventorillo del Chato **1** *C6*

Bars & clubs 🍸
Barabass **22** *C6*
Carbonera **27** *B5*
El Pay-Pay **21** *C5*
La Punta/Sala
  Anfiteatro **20** *A4*
Taberna La
  Hispaniola **30** *C6*

apart, they both date from around 400 BC and show that, even this late, the city still had important ties with its founders' homeland in the Eastern Mediterranean; throughout the ages, trade has been Cádiz's lifeline.

The **Roman** collection includes some reconstructed burials and displays of grave goods and funerary plaques. There are also some fine sculptures, particularly a large one of the (Andalucían) Emperor Trajan found at Baelo Claudia.

Upstairs, the **art section** has some excellent works. From the 15th century is a fine *Virgin Enthroned* by the Flemish Master of St Ursula, but the highlight is a fine series of Zurbarán's works from the Carthusian monastery at Jerez. The white-robed saints are painted with the artist's usual expressive treatment of cloth; the fact that he used monks as models make the figures especially realistic. Another series of monastery paintings here are by Francisco Osorio, who took on the job when his teacher, Murillo, died. Murillo is, however, represented by a Stigmata of St Francis. A portrait of a young Carlos II on horseback is a work of the underrated Asturian court painter Juan Carreño de Miranda; in the European section are two fine Giordanos and a small Rubens *Virgin and Child*, looking extremely Dutch. Among more recent works include a portrait by Ignacio Zuloaga, a Miró canvas, and the disturbing *Los Frutos*, by the postmodern tarifeño Guillermo Pérez Villalta.

Other places

Near the museum, the **Oratorio de la Santa Cueva** ① *Rosario s/n, T956-222262, Mon-Fri 1100-1300, 1700-2000, Sat and Sun 1000-1300, €3*, is a small chapel attached to El Rosario church. The two-tiered chapel, the lower sober neoclassical, the upper more extravagant late Baroque, contains three Goya canvases; serious works depicting the *Loaves and the Fishes*, the *Last Supper*, and the *Wedding Guest*.

South of Plaza San Antonio is another oratory, the **Oratorio San Felipe Neri** ① *C Santa Inés s/n, Mon-Sat 1000-1300, €2.50*. It was in here in 1812 that the historic Constitution was proclaimed and the *cortes* declared in session. The ellipsoid church has two tiers of balconies where the members sat. Plaques on the walls from all over the globe commemorate the event, which had an important impact on politics throughout the world. In the *retablo* is a fine *Immaculate Conception* by Murillo, being restored elsewhere at time of last research but due to return. Next door to the Oratorio is the **Museo de las Cortes de Cádiz** ① *Tue-Fri 0900-1800 (1900 summer), Sat and Sun 0900-1400, free*. Despite its name, there's no information on the constitution or the *cortes*, but the display of portraits and objects mostly come from that period. On the first floor is a striking wooden model of the city, commissioned by King Carlos III in the late 18th century.

Near here, it's worth seeking out the neo-Moorish **Gran Teatro Falla**, a striking building with striped horseshoe arches. A couple of blocks east of the Oratorio is the **Plaza de las Flores**, officially called the Plaza Topete and full of flower stalls; next to here is the market.

The **Torre de Tavira** ① *C Marqués del Real Tesoro 10, T956-212910, daily 1000-1800 (2000 summer, last entry 30 mins before closing), €5*, is a slim 18th-century tower with great views over the city. Another perspective is given by the fascinating **Camera Obscura**, a table-top on to which a magnified reflected image of the moving city is projected.

Beaches

The city's best and biggest beach is **Playa de la Victoria**, a long strip of clean sand in the new town. Bus No 1 runs here from the old town every five minutes or so; it's also just a short walk from the cathedral to the beginning of the strand. In summer it's a hive of activity with beach bars and *discotecas*; the streets behind are also full of eating and drinking options.

Cádiz listings

For sleeping and eating price codes and other relevant information, see pages 11-15.

⊙ Where to stay

Cádiz *p20, map p24*

There's plenty of good accommodation in the old town, mostly in the *hostal* category, but with a growing number of hotels too. Look out for the luxurious renovation of the **Casa del Almirante** tucked into the Barrio del Pópulo, scheduled to open as a luxury 5-star boutique hotel but still looking for investors to complete the transformation at time of the last research. The new town has several hotels near or on the beach but little in the budget category. Book ahead in summer and for Carnaval you'll need to reserve several months in advance; prices for even basic rooms are sky high at this time. The following price codes reflect summer rates; things drop substantially outside the beach season.

€€€€ Hotel Playa Victoria, Glorieta Ingeniero de la Cierva 4, T956-205100, www.palafoxhoteles.com. Luxurious and innovative, this striking large hotel sits in the most lively part of the new town, with the beach an elevator ride away and the best eating and drinking within a minute's stroll. All the rooms have a spacious balcony: the even numbers look out to the ocean, the odds face inland but give you a smidgen of sea view; there's also a pool with plenty of loungers, and various amenities throughout.

€€€ Hospedería Las Cortes de Cádiz, C San Francisco 9, T956-212668, www.hotel lascortes.com. In the heart of the old town, this spot makes a great base. Built around a central patio, it's all yellow ochre and white balcony rails, giving a cool, light feel. The rooms are inviting, with high wooden bedheads and modern comforts like digital TV and a/c. Pick an exterior room if you can: the noise from the bustling street is worth it

for the extra light. There are views from the roof as well as a gym and sauna.

€€€ Hotel Spa Cádiz Plaza, Glorieta Ingeniero La Cierva 3, T956-079190, www. cadizplaza.com. This relative newcomer offers bright and sparky rooms, some with sea views and balconies, in optimistic colour schemes just a few metres from the beach. Spa complex and upbeat and helpful staff. Bikes and beach gear for hire.

€€€ Parador Atlántico, Av Duque de Nájera 9, T956-226905, www.parador.es. With an excellent location at the tip of the Cádiz promontory and the Barrio de la Viña's enticing eating options in easy reach, this will hopefully live up to its position when an extensive renovation is completed in 2012. Many of the rooms have sea views, and there's an outdoor pool looking over the Atlantic. It may rise in price category when it re-opens.

€€ Hostal Bahía, C Plocia 5, T956-259061, www.hostalbahiacadiz.com. Right in the heart of things near Plaza San Juan de Dios, this small *hostal* is one of the best options in the old town. All rooms have a/c, TV, balcony and modern bathroom, and the management are helpful. If rooms are a touch spartan for the price, it's worth it for the location. You may be able to haggle a better price.

€€ Hostal Canalejas, C Colón 5, T956-264113, www.hostalcanalejas.com. This *hostal* offers more facilities than most of the choices in this central cluster of accommodation, with a lift, off-street parking (at a cost), and Wi-Fi. The rooms have a/c and heating, though they'll never host the world cat-swinging championships.

€€ Hostal Fantoni, C Flamenco 5, T956-282704, www.hostalfantoni.es. Handily close to the tourist office, tucked up a side street, this place offers darkish modern rooms with a/c, heating and good bathrooms. It's built around a tiled patio, and there are some well-thumbed paperbacks to browse. Noise echoes through the building, so light sleepers might look elsewhere. Some rooms are a lot better than others; try to avoid the first one on the left as you go upstairs or the one at the top of the spiral staircase.

€€ **Hotel Argantonio**, C Argantonio 3, T956-211640, www.hotelargantonio.com. This hotel is a sound choice. It occupies a solid old house in a narrow old town street, and has Moorish-inspired decor and very friendly service. Offers good value for this level of comfort. Rates include breakfast. Recommended.

€€ **Hotel Regio**, Av Ana de Viya 11, T956-279331, www.hotelregiocadiz.com. One of the better options in the beach zone, this modern and functional hotel has well-equipped rooms and competent staff. Rooms on the front side can be noisy but also have the bustle of life on the main road to observe.

€ **Casa Caracol**, C Suárez de Salazar 4, T956-261166, www.hostel-casacaracol.com. In a narrow street in the old town, handy for the train station, this backpacker hostel is a cheerful place that wins more points for atmosphere than facilities. It's friendly, but comforts like decent mattresses and lockers are absent. Sleeping is in noisy 4-bed dorms (€15-20) and there's a roof terrace with hammocks. Book ahead. Hard to find; look for the snail sign.

€ **Cuatro Naciones**, C Plocia 3, T956-255539. Simple but clean rooms with tartan blankets in a great central location. There's a modern shared bathroom, the place is surprisingly quiet, and the management are friendly. Under different management and in various locations, **Cuatro Naciones** has been a *fonda* for over 150 years.

Camping

The nearest campsites to Cádiz are in Chiclana, about 25 km away.

Cádiz *p20, map p24*

Cádiz is among Andalucía's best places to eat, with seafood restaurants jostling with lively tapas bars. The old town's best choices are somewhat scattered, but the area around Plaza de la Mina, especially C Zorilla, is good for tapas, as is the Paseo Marítimo on the beach in the new town.

€€€ **El Faro**, C San Félix 15, T956-229916, www.elfarodecadiz.com. This whitewashed little place with a row of tavern lamps outside looks like a humble enough spot at first glance, but is actually one of the region's most celebrated fish restaurants, and deservedly so. The menu and wine list are excellent; some recommendations include *rape con pasas y jerez* (monkfish stewed in raisins and sherry), any of the rice dishes, overflowing with fishy flavours, and the *paté de cabracho*, a tasty scorpionfish mousse. Prices are reasonable for this level of quality; there's also a tapas bar where you can enjoy cheaper but equally perfect fare.

€€ **Arte Serrano**, Paseo Marítimo 2, T956-277258. In a large building on the beachfront promenade, this is one of Puerta de Tierra's most visited spots. In the massive but warm space, you can sit down and enjoy the seafood or browse the extensive tapas menu standing at the long bar. Tapas range from €1.50 to €3 and are delicious. There's also a big covered terrace.

€€ **Casa Tino**, C Rosa 25, T956-214313, www.tinodecadiz.com. A small and neatly fitted bar with bright lights and hanging onions, pictures of horses and black and white photos of Cádiz personalities. The tapas to try here are seafood and stews; the latter fill a range of metal pans sitting temptingly on the bar and include venison and bull's tail. Among the fishy offerings, try the fresh *ortiguillas* (sea anemones) from the bay if they're on. Combine this with nearby Taberna Casa Manteca and the bar of El Faro restaurant for a wonderful tapas trio in this traditional fishing *barrio*.

€€ El Balandro, Alameda Apodaca 22, T956-220992, www.restaurantebalandro. com. A large and sophisticated seafood restaurant and tapas bar with a comfortable dining area overlooking the bay. The fresh local fish and salads are tasty and the prices are very reasonable for the quality. At the bar there's courteous service and fine wines by the glass, among the busy buzz of upmarket *gaditanos*. Tapas here are €4-6 but 2 of them are a meal.

€€ El Ventorrillo del Chato, Ctra Cádiz-San Fernando s/n, T956-257116, www. ventorrilloelchato.com. By the beach just outside of the city, this place has plenty of character and history but doesn't rest on those. Excellent seafood with innovative touches and warm, friendly service make this worth seeking out. Head out of Cádiz, taking the San Fernando road, and you'll see it on the right shortly after leaving the urban area. Recommended.

€€ Mesón Cumbres Mayores, C Zorilla 4, T856-072242, www.mesoncumbres mayores.com. This ultra-atmospheric spot is as good as it ever was, and is one of Andalucía's most lovable tapas bars. It oozes character from creaking wooden beams, lively range of customers, hanging ham and garlic. The staff are on the ball, and will recommend from their long tapas list. *Diablillos* are dates wrapped in bacon; the pork *secreto* or a *carrillada* are also worth trying. It's also a fine place to sit down and eat, with efficient service at the tables out the back. You'll never try tastier pork cuts, with the *entrecot* delicious and the mixed grill for two a good way to try a variety. Recommended.

€€ Puntaparrilla, Glorieta de Cortadura s/n, T956-201332. One of the city's best options for a meaty meal, this barn of a place is festooned with hanging hams and has warm wooden decor. The menu has numerous types and cuts of meat, with excellent roasts and grills in massive portions. Right at the end of the Paseo Marítimo almost at the edge of the city.

€€ Taberna San Francisco I, Plaza San Francisco s/n, T956-212597. Open 0900-0200. An upmarket red-ceilinged corner bar built in stone and brick with an inviting wooden terrace on the square. There are original *raciones* such as moussaka served on outsized white plates; there are also mixed platters typical of the province. Several vegetarian options, and a good but pricey wine list. Also a nice spot for coffee.

€ Bahía, Av Ramón de Carranza 29, T956-281166. One of the Cádiz classics, this is the best of a short string of bars opposite the passenger docks near the tourist office. It's famous among locals for its pork ribs and fish in saffron sauce, and also has a shaded terrace outside and as-it-should-be service.

€ Casa Taberna Manteca, C Corralón de los Carros s/n, T956-213603. One of the city's favourite tapas bars, this lively spot is decked out with flamenco and bullfighting photos. The tapas are all *chacinas* (hams, sausage, cured pork, cheeses), and are served on squares of greaseproof paper. The ham melts like butter in the mouth and the service is keen and friendly. For atmosphere there are few better bars in the province. Highly recommended.

€ Freiduría Las Flores, C Brasil s/n and Plaza de Topete 4, T956-289378. Las Flores is a Cádiz institution, with locations in the old and new towns. What they do is fried seafood, and they do it exceptionally well and cheerily. A mixed bag costs €4.80 for 250 g to take away and munch on the beach; you can also graze on tapas at the bar or sit down for larger portions.

€ Gotinga, Plaza Mentidero 15, T856-070580. Open Mon-Fri 0900-0100, Sat 1300-0100. A warm and welcoming little restaurant with cool yellow walls and a terrace. They do tapas but really focus on a handful of fresh fish and pasta dishes, which are prepared with tender loving care. The menu ranges across various countries, including such inventive fusions as pork with tsatziki. There's plenty of veggie choice, good-value daily fish specials, and they mix a fine cocktail too. It's deservedly popular, and has had to take over the house next door to fit everybody in.

€ La Gorda te da de Comer, C General Luque 1, T607-539946. A busy and friendly bar with chatty staff, brightly painted walls, wooden tables and a touch of the 1970s thrown in. La Gorda (the fat lady) turns out to be the gay chef, and he turns out generous tapas of typical Cádiz dishes for low prices. The proof of the pudding is that not many tapas bars have queues outside waiting for opening time and a scramble for tables. There's another branch at Marqués de Valdeiñigo 4 nearby, with the same decor and food.

Cafés

El Tendero, Av Ramón de Carranza 24, T659-939837. A cheerful and warm café opposite the port that does a soothing hot chocolate and a range of pastries and croissants. It manages to be both spacious and cosy at the same time. Converts itself seamlessly into a popular evening tapas bar.

Habana Café, C Rosario 21. In the centre of the shopping district, this light white space offers a serene spot for an early evening drink. Things liven up a little later and the barman makes very decent mojitos and other cocktails.

La Catedral, Plaza de la Catedral 9, T956-252184. A fine spot to sit on a fake wooden terrace in a pretty square with palm trees, dominated by the cathedral facade. Despite the location, it's not a tourist trap and also serves great quality tapas and full meals (**€€**). The terrace is a good spot to check emails on your laptop with the city's free Wi-Fi network.

🎵 Bars and clubs

Cádiz p20, map p24
Cádiz has excellent nightlife all year round. In summer, the focus is on the beach, while for the rest of the year it's around Punta San Felipe. This pier jutting into the bay has many bars as well as the city's best *discoteca*. In the new town, the Paseo Marítimo beyond C Brasil has many bars, as does C General Muñoz Arenillas. On the beach in summer are numerous *chiringuitos*, which pump their music late and loud.

Barabass, C Muñoz Arenillas 4, T856-079026, www.barabasscadiz.es. Open 1800 to 0500 or 0700 at weekends. With chill-out music in the evenings turning into house beats later on, this stylish venue with dark stone tiles and slick modern decor gets packed at weekends. There's a door policy but it's not cliquey, and is one of the best nightlife options in Cádiz any day of the week.

Carbonera, C Marqués de Cádiz 1, T956-272800. This sort of bar is disappearing in Spain, replaced by more fashion-conscious watering holes. It defines authentic, with its faded tiles, weathered old men and barrels of simple, tasty, and cheap *finos* and *manzanillas*; an exercise in simplicity a few steps from the town hall square.

El Pay-Pay, C Silencio 1, T956-252543. Wed-Sat from 2200, also Sun and Tue in summer. Once an elegant society café, then a high-class brothel, this place has been reopened as a bar and music venue. There are frequent live shows, ranging from flamenco to comedy to jazz and blues, as well as exhibitions of photos and paintings. Whatever's on, there are always plenty of people drinking in the characterful interior until late. Recommended.

La Punta/Sala Anfiteatro, Punta San Felipe s/n, www.salaanfiteatro.com. Cádiz's best *discoteca* is open Thu-Sat all year. It is in fact an amphitheatre in shape (hence the name) and gets busy around 0300-0400 until closing time at 0700. Entry can be tricky on Sat night, so it's worth turning up early to beat the crowds. The €10 fee includes a drink. Music is light dance to Spanish pop hits. In the same strip are many disco-bars.

Taberna La Nueva Hispaniola, Paseo Marítimo 23, T956-258458. Set sail for the Spanish Main! This fabulous beachside bar recreates the glory days of the pirate, but is

Cádiz Carnaval

Cádiz has always half faced away from Spain, out to sea, and it's no surprise that the carnival here is very different to those in the rest of the peninsula. Part of this can be ascribed to the independent *gaditanos* themselves, and part to the extensive contact and interchange Cádiz enjoyed with cities such as Venice and Genoa.

The party in Cádiz goes on for nine days, although it centres on Shrove Tuesday. Everyone wears fancy dress and takes to the streets for much drinking and merriment. There's plenty of live music and other performances, but the most famous come from the *agrupaciones*, groups of musicians and comedians who satirize contemporary political figures and events. The best-loved are the *chirigotas*, choirs of 10 singers accompanied by guitar, bombo and a wooden box used as a drum. Their songs are usually the most biting and sung to popular folk

tunes. During the week, these groups, as well as roaming the streets, compete for a prestigious prize in the Falla theatre. There are plenty of impromptu musical gatherings on the streets too, whether it be flamenco or some of Cádiz's more exotic rhythms such as sambas or creole beats. There are several parades, and a daily ear-splitting explosion of firecrackers in Plaza San Juan de Dios known as *La Toronda* (the thunderclap).

It's difficult and expensive to get accommodation in Cádiz over *Carnaval*. It should be booked several months or more in advance. Even nearby cities like El Puerto de Santa María are usually full. If you can't get a bed, it's not a big deal. Plenty of people stay up all night and then get the train back to Jerez or Sevilla, only to return for the next night's festivities. The atmosphere on this party train can be colourful in itself.

---

anything but tacky. Loads of effort has been put into making it feel like a cross between a galleon and a bar of the era, with beer served in tankards. They also do tasty food.

🎭 Entertainment

Cádiz *p20, map p24*
Flamenco
Centro Municipal de Arte Flamenco La Merced, Plaza Merced s/n, T956-285189, www.cadiz.es. This performance and rehearsal space normally has a couple of performances a week, most of them free.
La Cava, C Antonio López 16, T956-211866, www.flamencolacava.com. Has a good flamenco show on Tue, Thu and Sat (also Wed and Fri Jul-Sep). It's quite a dressy spot. Entry to the show is €22; this includes a drink.
Peña Flamenca La Perla de Cádiz, C Carlos Ollero s/n, T956-259101, www.perladecadiz. com. By the sea at the edge of the old

town, this spacious venue has regular live performances: check the website for upcoming events.

🎉 Festivals

Cádiz *p20, map p24*
Feb/Mar The city is world-famous for its riotous 9-day **Carnaval** (www.carnavalde cadiz.com; see box, above).
7 Oct a smaller fiesta to celebrate the city's patron, **La Virgen del Rosario**.

⚓ What to do

Cádiz *p20, map p24*
Bike hire
Urban Bike Cádiz, C Marqués de Valdeiñigo 4, T856-170164, Magistral Cabrera 7, T664-081381, www.urbanbikecadiz.es. In the new town, bikes for €8/12 half day/day. Ring ahead for weekend rentals.

Football

Although outside the top flight at time of writing, going to watch Cádiz football team is one of Spain's more memorable sporting experiences. In contrast to many Spanish teams' hardcore fans, the Cádiz support is leftwing, committedly anti-racist, and prefer their team to lose pretty than to win ugly. The stadium, the Ramón Carranza, is in the new town, close to the beach. The fans' relentless good humour and sportsmanship give the games a fiesta atmosphere. **Estadio Carranza**, T956-070165, www.cadizcf.com.

⊖ Transport

Cádiz *p20, map p24*
Bus
The principal bus station is just off Plaza de España, T956-807059. The main company is Comes, who run hourly buses to **Sevilla** (1 hr 45 mins). **Málaga** is targeted 6 times a day (4 hrs); there are also several daily buses to **Granada** and a couple to **Córdoba** and **Ronda**. **Madrid** is served 3-6 times daily (8 hrs) by Secorbus, who run from Plaza Helios near the football stadium and the Carranza bridge.

Within Cádiz province, **Comes** runs more than hourly to **Jerez** (40 mins) and El Puerto de Santa María (30 mins), 5 a day to **Tarifa** (1 hr 30 mins), 10 to **Algeciras** (with 3 continuing to **La Línea** for Gibraltar), and 6-10 to **Barbate**, as well as other coastal destinations. Inland, **Arcos de la Frontera** is reached 3-6 times daily, and **Medina Sidonia** 5 times.

Los Amarillos, T956-285852, runs from opposite the tourist office on Av Ramón de Carranza to **Chipiona** via **Sanlúcar de Barrameda** (1 hr 15 mins) 11 times on weekdays and 5 times on weekends. They also run 2-4 buses to **Ubrique** (2 hrs 15 mins) via **Arcos de la Frontera** (1 hr).

Car rental

Bahía, Plaza de Sevilla s/n, T956-271895, www.bahiarentacar.com.

Ferry

There's a catamaran service that nips across the bay to El Puerto de Santa María 5-10 times daily, 30 mins, €2.20 each way.

Trasmediterránea, Av Ramón de Carranza 26, T956-292811, www.trasmediterranea.es, runs a weekly ferry to the **Canary Islands**, stopping at **Santa Cruz de Tenerife**, **Las Palmas** and **Santa Cruz de la Palma**. Currently leaving Cádiz on Tue, it takes 38 hrs to Las Palmas and about 48 hrs to Tenerife. The crossing tends to be rough, and it's not great value compared with the flight deals available.

Train

Cádiz's train station is by the port near the centre of town, T902-240202. There are 10-12 daily trains to **Sevilla** (1 hr 45 mins) via **Puerto de Santa María** and **Jerez**. Several of these connect with trains to **Málaga**, **Granada**, or **Almería** in Dos Hermanas; 1 continues to **Jaén** (5 hrs). There are 2 daily fast trains for **Madrid** (5 hrs). **El Puerto de Santa María** and **Jerez** are also served by regular *cercanía* trains every 30 mins. The trip to El Puerto takes 35 mins, and to Jerez 45-50 mins.

⊙ Directory

Cádiz *p20, map p24*
Internet Many places around the centre of Cádiz are geared up as free Wi-Fi zones. **Medical services** For emergencies, Hospital Universitario, Av Ana de Viya 21, T956-002100; for non-emergencies, go to a Centro de Salud, such as the one on C Cervantes 9, T956-225469. **Post** Plaza Topete s/n, T956-210511.

North from Cádiz

Across the bay from Cádiz, the sherry-producing town of El Puerto de Santa María is but a short boat trip away. It's a favourite spot for a seafood lunch. With several notable buildings, this town is an important bullfighting centre. Further west, on the edge of the inspiring Coto Doñana wetlands, Sanlúcar de Barrameda is also a centre for sherry. Sanlúcar was where Magellan finally set sail from, and it still has the feel of a colonial-era port.

El Puerto de Santa María → *For listing, see pages 45-52.*

Across the bay from Cádiz, El Puerto de Santa María wears two hats. Its elegant old town testifies to its days as a burgeoning trading and steamer port – Columbus' 1492 flagship, the *Santa María*, was from here – while its fish restaurants make a popular and hard-to-beat lunch excursion from Cádiz, Jerez or Sevilla. In summer, though, the nearby beaches rocks to some of Spain's raunchiest nightlife. It is also a sherry town, home to well-known brands as Osborne and Terry, whose cavernous *bodegas* impart their distinctive fragrance to the narrow streets.

Arriving in El Puerto de Santa María

One of the best ways to get to the town is by boat from Cádiz. The old town lies on the northwest bank of the Río Guadalete, which flows into the Bahía de Cádiz. The town's two beaches are on the bay: Playa de la Puntilla on the city side, and the longer Playa de Valdelagrana on the other side of the river. Several buses link the beaches with the old centre. → *See Transport, page 52.*

The town's excellent **tourist office** ① *near the boat dock at C Luna 22, T956-542413, www.turismoelpuerto.com, daily 1000-1400, 1700-1930 Oct-Apr, 1800-2000 May-Sep,* provides maps with details of a walk taking in the main sights, helpfully marked on the pavement with a red stripe. It also has useful printed sheets of accommodation, transport, tapas routes, etc. Free walking tours leave here at 1100 on Saturday.

Places in El Puerto de Santa María

First constructed by the Moors in the 10th century, **Castillo de San Marcos** ① *Plaza Alfonso X El Sabio s/n, T956-851751, Tue-Sat by prior arrangement, €5,* was rebuilt by Alfonso X in the 13th century, an event he refers to in one of his many writings. The castle has restored heraldic friezes, dogtooth battlements, and Marian inscriptions decorating the walls and towers. The impressive wooden door opens for guided tours that must be prebooked; they run in English and Spanish. It's worth a visit to see the chapel built over a mosque, whose foundations it preserves. It has a fine 13th-century Gothic sculpture of Santa María de España.

The **Plaza de España** is dominated by the parish church of **Nuestra Señora de los Milagros** ① *T956-851716, Mon-Fri 0830-1245, 1800-2030, Sat 0830-1200, 1800-2030, Sun 0830-1345, 1830-2030, free,* a late 15th-century Gothic building with flying buttresses and various 17th-century additions. These include the ornate Plateresque/Baroque portal, with intricate vegetal and cherubic decoration, a tympanum with niches holding

El Puerto de Santa María

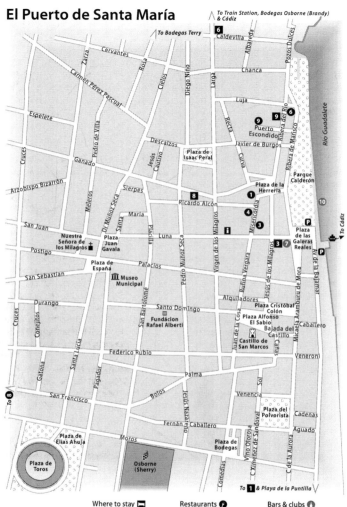

To Train Station, Bodegas Osborne (Brandy) & Cádiz

To Bodegas Terry

6 Caldevilla

Cervantes

Zarza

Carmen Pérez Pascual

Rosa

Cielos

Diego Niño

Larga

Chanca

Albareda

Pozos Dulces

Luja

Espelete

Pedro de Villa

Descalzos

Recta

Ribera del Río

9 Puerto Escondido

9 **6**

Jesús Cautivo

Plaza de Isaac Peral

Javier de Burgos

Cruva

Ribera de Marisco

Río Guadalete

Ganado

Sierpes

Plaza de la Herrería

Parque Calderón

Arzobispo Bizarrón

Meteros

Dr. Muñoz Seca

Santa

María

Plácida

Ricardo Alcón

8

Misericordia

1

4

Virgen de los Milagros

10

To Cádiz

San Juan

Luna

i

3

Nuestra Señora de los Milagros

Plaza Juan Gavala

Pedro Muñoz Seca

Plaza de las Galeras Reales

Postigo

Plaza de España

Palacios

Rufina Vergara

Calle de los Milagros

3 **7**

San Sebastián

III Museo Municipal

Durango

Santo Domingo

Alquiladores

Plaza Cristóbal Colón

Micaela Aramburu de Mora

Conejitos

Cruces

San Bartolomé

Fundáción Rafael Alberti

Plaza Alfonso El Sabio

Bajada del Castillo

Caballero

Santa Lucía

Gatona

Pagador

Federico Rubio

Juan de la Cosa

Jesús de los Milagros

î Castillo de San Marcos

Veneron

Palma

Sol

Durango

San Francisco

Bolos

Jesús Nazareno

Venencia

Plaza del Polvorista

Cadenas

Aguado

Fernán Caballero

Moros

Plaza de Bodegas

Vino Otoro

Ximénez de Sandoval

C. de la Aurora

Comedias

To **1** *& Playa de la Puntilla*

Plaza de Elías Ahuja

Plaza de Toros

Osborne (Sherry)

N

100 metres

100 yards

To **8**

Where to stay 🛏	Restaurants 🍴	Bars & clubs 🍸
Camping Playa Las Dunas **1**	Aponiente **9**	El Loco de la Ribera **7**
Casa de los Leones **2**	El Faro de El Puerto **8**	La Pontona **10**
Casa del Regidor **9**	La Antigua **4**	
Hostal Esperanza **3**	La Bodeguilla del Bar Jamón **3**	
Hostal Loreto **8**	La Taberna del Puerto **6**	
Los Cántaros **5**	Mesón del Asador **1**	
Monasterio San Miguel **6**		

sculptures of Mary (who is standing atop the town's castle) and the Evangelists, and a strange bearded God atop it all. The side door is an equally elaborate Gothic affair with curious protruding piers. The sea air isn't helping the limestone, which unfortunately is becoming severely corroded.

The **Fundación Rafael Alberti** ① *C Santo Domingo 25, T956-850711, Tue-Sun 1030-1400 (closed weekends from mid-Jun to mid-Sep), €5*, is situated in the house where the 20th-century *portuense* writer lived as a child. There's a collection of objects and documents from his life. A Communist and friend of Federico García Lorca, Alberti was one of the important figures of the Generación del '27, and most famous for his lyrical autobiography *La Arboleta Perdida* (The Lost Grove). Alberti fled at the end of the Civil War, and stayed in exile until after the death of Franco in 1975.

The large **bullring** ① *T956-541578, Tue-Sun 1100-1330, 1730-1900, free, high-quality fights every Sun in Jul and Aug*, looking like a brick Colosseum, is one of the more important in Spain; indeed an inscription by Joselito claims that if you haven't seen bulls here, you don't know bullfighting. When there's no fight on you can wander in and have a look round the ring, which holds 15,000.

Bodegas

The tourist office will supply a list of the town's wineries that are open for visiting. Most of them require a prior phone call to book. The best known is undoubtedly **Osborne** ① *sherry bodega, T956-869100, www.osborne.es, tours by prior appointment Mon-Fri 1030 in English, 1200 Spanish, Sat 1100 English, 1200 Spanish, €7.50; brandy bodega Ctra NIV Km 651, near the train station, T956-854228, open by prior appointment*. Founded in the 18th century, the company's 90-odd giant metal black bulls dotted around the country's main roads have become a well-known symbol of Spain. A law forbidding roadside advertising threatened their complete removal in the 1990s (the logo had already been removed for the same reason), but the Supreme Court decreed them as part of the nation's cultural heritage, so they are here to stay. There are two *bodegas* in town, one for the sherry, and one for the brandy.

Another big outfit geared to visits is **Terry** ① *C Toneleros s/n, T956-857700, www. bodegasterry.com, bilingual Spanish/English visits Mon-Fri 1030 and 1230, Sat 1200, €8, no prior appointment necessary*, whose attractive *bodega* tour includes some fine white Carthusian horses pulling a carriage if there are enough visitors.

Chipiona

Past the huge yachting marina of Puerto Sherry and Rota, with a US naval base, Chipiona, 9 km from Sanlúcar, is a cheery seaside town with fine beaches. It's notable for its lighthouse, whose 344 steps can be climbed for the views.

Sanlúcar de Barrameda → *For listing, see pages 45-52.*

In its heyday this delightful town was an important port for the Americas and was once even touted as a potential capital of Spain. Its narrow streets still proudly bear the mansions of the town's pomp, while Sanlúcar is also famous for serving some of Andalucía's best seafood. A happy coincidence this, for Sanlúcar produces arguably Spain's finest accompaniment to fresh shellfish, *manzanilla*, a light sherry tangy with the taste of the sea breeze. From Sanlúcar you can take trips to Coto Doñana, see page 51.

Arriving in Sanlúcar de Barrameda

The town is divided into an upper and lower *barrio*, with most of the action down below, around the central Plaza de Cabildo. On the beach 1 km along from the lower town is **Bajo de Guía**, traditionally a fishermen's demesne and now location of excellent restaurants. Sanlúcar has limited parking, tight corners and a fiendish one-way system, so park in one of the underground car parks or near the beach and explore the town on foot.

The **tourist office** ① *Calzada de Ejército s/n, T956-366110, summer daily 1000-1400, 1800-2000, winter Mon-Fri 1000-1400, 1600-1800, Sat 1000-1245, Sun 1000-1400,* is located on the long avenue descending to the beach from near Plaza de Cabildo. It's well organized, with various info sheets on the town. There's also an information desk in the Fábrica de Hielo (see page 37); book trips to the Parque Nacional Coto Doñana here. ▸ *See Transport, page 52.*

Background

Sanlúcar was entrusted after the reconquest to Guzmán El Bueno (of Tarifa fame) in the late 13th century. Still resident here today are his descendants, the Dukes of Medina Sidonia. Sanlúcar's superb position facing the Atlantic meant it became an important port once the Americas had been discovered, when wealthy merchants and chandlers built the mansions that still ennoble the town. Columbus sailed from here on his third voyage in 1498, and this was the last place Magellan set foot in Spain. Leaving Sanlúcar on 20 September 1519 with five ships and over 200 men, he attempted to circumnavigate the world. Only one of the ships, the *Victoria*, made it home, three years later. This was skippered by Juan Sebastián Elcano (Elkano), as Magellan himself only got as far as the Philippines before dying in an ill-advised intervention in a local conflict. Sanlúcar, a wealthy and important city in the 16th century, began to decline, but by the 19th

Sanlúcar de Barrameda

Río Guadalquivir

Boats to Coto Doñana

Nuestra Señora del Carmen

BAJO DE GUIA

Fábrica de Hielo

Paseo Marítimo

Av de Bajo de Guía

Av Carbo Noval

Av Guadalquivir

Av Cerro Falón

Padre Cuetas

Av de la Circunvalación

C de San Nicolás

Trasbolsa

Bolsa

Rubio

Juan XXIII

Calzada del Ejército

Fco Pizarro

Santo Tomás

Infanta Beatriz

Banda Playa

BARRIO BAJO

Trasbolsa

Templo de San Francisco

To Bonanza

Carril de San Diego

Beregüela

C Mar

Diego Bean Diego

Santo Domingo

Don Claudio

To Bus Station

Tartaneros

Plaza del Cabildo

Ancha

Santa Ana

Chanca

Plaza San Roque

Museo del Mar

San Juan

Palacio de los Duques Medina Sidonia

Castillo de Santiago

Barbadillo

la Cigarrera

Nuestra Señora de la O

Palma

Gitanos

Anbarch

Las Covachas

Palacio de Orléans-Borbón

Cuartel

Escuelas

Plaza la Paz

Caballeros

N

100 metres
100 yards

Where to stay ⬛
Barrameda 7
Hostal Blanca Paloma 3
Palacio de los Duques
  Medina Sidonia 6
Pensión la Bohemia 1
Posada de Palacio 5
Tartaneros 4

Restaurants ●
Bar Juanito 4
Cantina 6
Casa Balbino 5
Casa Bigote 1
Despacho de Vinos
  Las Palomas 2
Heladería Bornay 3
La Lonja 8
La Taberna Taurina 7

Bars & clubs ●
Bajo de Guía 67 9

and 20th centuries it became a fashionable resort. Today, fishing, *manzanilla* and tourism keep the town in euros.

Places in Sanlúcar de Barrameda

The lower town is centred on the pretty Plaza del Cabildo, which is surrounded by terraced cafés, as is the neighbouring Plaza San Roque. From here, you can climb Calle Bretones, which passes the lively food market and Las Covachas, a curious Gothic arcade that is decorated with sea monsters; its original use is unknown.

Continuing up the hill, you get a fine view over the rooftops, one of which is kitted out as the deck of a ship. This is the eccentric **Museo del Mar** ① *C Truco 4, T956-367396, daily 1000-2200, €2*, also called Museo de los Caracoles, a private collection of beachcomber curios such as shark jaws (up for sale) and over 80,000 seashells. The entrance just is off Plaza San Roque; you'll be shown around by the owner, who will probably be the most unusual person you'll meet in Sanlúcar.

Further up the street, passing the elaborate **Teatro Merced**, housed in an old convent, you come to the **Palacio de Orléans-Borbón** ① *Cuesta de Belén s/n, Mon-Fri 0800-1430, plus Sat and Sun 1030-1300 with free guided visit*, a summer palace built by the Duke and Duchess of Montpensier (the sister of Queen Isabel II of Spain). Now the town hall, it is a fantastic neo-Moorish creation built at the height of Alhambra romanticism. Have a look at the stunning porch and the central patio.

Turning left, you'll come to the church of **Nuestra Señora de la O** ① *open only at 1930 for mass*, a 14th-century building with a striking main doorway possessed of fine *mudéjar* stonework above a Gothic arch. The round belltower is decorated with paintings of saints; inside, note the star-patterned *mudéjar* ceiling and 16th-century frescoes.

Next to here is the **Palacio de los Duques Medina Sidonia** ① *Plaza Condes de Niebla s/n, T956-360161, www.fcmedinasidonia.com, tours Sun only 1100 and 1200 by prior appointment, €3.50, café open Mon-Fri 0830-1400, 1530-2100, Sat 1530-0200, Sun 0830-0200*, an elegant white building mostly dating from the 19th century, but with some chambers remaining from the 15th-century original. It still belongs to the ducal family who are directly descended from the Guzmán family who used to rule the town. There's an important archive of historical documents here, as well as numerous works of art and antique furniture. There are also some rooms available to rent (see page 46) and a rather charming café.

Further along, the **Castillo de Santiago** ① *C Cava de Castillo s/n, T956-088329, www.castillodesantiago.com, guided tours Tue-Sat at 1100, 1200, 1300, plus 2000 and 2100 summer €5*, was built in the 15th century into part of the city walls. It as here that Fernando and Isabel stayed when they visited the town. The hexagonal keep and various Isabelline Gothic details are the most impressive features.

The beach is a 10-minute walk from Plaza del Cabildo and is pleasant, with fine clean sand. It's the scene of a curious spectacle in August, when serious **horse races** are conducted along it. They have all the trimmings: betting tents, binoculars and prize money (check www.carrerassanlucar.es for dates and details).

Turning right along the waterfront, you'll soon come to **Bajo de Guía**. This was once the fishermen's quarter and still has a few boats, although most of the serious fishing goes on out of nearby Bonanza. There's a string of excellent seafood restaurants here, a fishermen's chapel to **Nuestra Señora del Carmen**, as well as the **Fábrica de Hielo** ① *T956-381635, daily 0900-2000 (1900 winter), free*, a former ice factory that now has a tourist information booth and the booking office for boat trips to the Coto Doñana national park (see What to do, page 51). There's also a display on different zones of the national park, and a good exhibition upstairs on the history of the region and the voyage of Magellan and his crew; there's a model of the only ship from that expedition to make it back, the *Victoria*.

The *Real Fernando* is a chunky old boat that runs trips from Sanlúcar across to the Coto Doñana (see What to do, page 51).

Bodegas

There are several *manzanilla bodegas* in town, two of which can be visited without phoning ahead. The smallest, oldest, and most delightful to visit is right in the heart of town tucked up a side street near the food market. **Bodegas La Cigarrera** ① *Plaza Madre de Dios s/n, T956-381285, www.bodegaslacigarrera.com, Mon-Sat 1000-1500, €3 per person*, is housed in part of a former convent, and its atmospheric barrel vaults surround a pretty patio. It was founded in 1758 and is still run by the same family. Short visits leave on the half-hour and explain plenty about *manzanilla*. Their *fino* is unfiltered and delicious; you get a taste at the end of the tour.

With a production dozens of times larger, **Barbadillo** ① *next to the castle, T956-385500, www.barbadillo.com, tours Tue-Sat 1100 (English), 1200 and 1300 (Spanish), €3; winemaking display Mon-Sat 1100-1500*, offers tours as well as a winemaking museum.

Around Sanlúcar de Barrameda

If you don't manage to visit the Parque Nacional Coto Doñana itself, you can get some idea of it (and see a multitude of waterbirds) by driving a circular route along this side of the Guadalquivir estuary. From Sanlúcar, head northeast 23 km to the town of Trebujena. From the centre of Trebujena, follow signs (you may have to ask) to the estuary (*las marismas*). Just past **Chozas Marismeñas** hotel, 6 km from town, the road ends at the water. Here, you can turn left along a poor road, flanked by bird-rich wetlands, which will eventually lead back to Bonanza and Sanlúcar. Cut through Parque Dunar, an expanse of sand dunes, on your way back.

Jerez de la Frontera → *For listing, see pages 45-52. Phone code: 956. Population: 208,896.*

Quiet, genteel Jerez is quite a contrast to nearby Cádiz. Larger than its provincial capital, and Andalucía's fifth largest city, it rarely feels like it. The city is famous for its sherry, the wine that takes its name from the place (see box, page 43). Jerez is also known as an important centre of flamenco and of horsemanship; the dancing white Carthusian mounts have a training base here (see box, opposite). Jerez is also home to a faster steed; it's the venue for the Spanish motorcycling Grand Prix, which sometimes coincides with the town's lively May *feria*.

Arriving in Jerez de la Frontera

Getting there and around Jerez is easily reached by public transport from either Sevilla or Cádiz. The train and bus stations are adjacent at the eastern end of town, a 15-minute walk from the centre. Jerez's airport is 8 km northeast. ►► *See Transport, page 52.*

Local bus No 10 runs from the train and bus stations into town. There are infrequent airport buses; otherwise a taxi will only cost around €13. Most of Jerez's sights are within walking distance of the centre, but for the farther flung ones jump on a local bus in the Plaza del Arenal. The tourist office has a route map.

Best time to visit Visiting during the Feria de Caballo, Jerez's main fiesta in the first half of May, is recommended, but you'll struggle to find accommodation. Many revellers just come from Sevilla or Cádiz on the train and stay up all night. Jerez gets very hot in summer, so spring and autumn are the most suitable times for a visit.

All the pretty horses

In Moorish times, there were two basic types of horses in the peninsula: the heavy northern mounts, originally brought by the Celts and of Germanic bloodlines, and the lighter *berberisco* horses of the south, elegant beasts suitable for light cavalry. These were originally brought across from North Africa but were resident in the peninsula well before the Moors' arrival. After the Reconquest, the Castillian crown wished to merge the two species to create an all-purpose Spanish horse. This duly happened, but a few landowners refused to surrender their pure Andalucían horses and gave them into the care of Carthusian monks, who maintained a breeding programme of the elegant creatures that some say are descended from the unicorn, as a bony protrusion on the muzzle is a common genetic trait. Thus the horses came to be known as Carthusians, or *Cartujanos*, and have been very highly prized ever since for their beauty and grace.

Although the monasteries were disentailed in the 1830s, a few breeders kept the line going. They are often fastidiously groomed and dressed and highly trained to 'dance' or walk sideways, a spectacle you can see at *corridas de rejones* (horseback bullfights), or at the Real Escuela de Arte Ecuestre in Jerez, a city historically linked with these horses.

Tourist information The city **tourist office** ① *C Larga 39, T956-338874, www.turismojerez. com, Mon-Fri 0900-1500, 1630-1830 (1730-2030 summer), Sat and Sun 0930-1430 (1530 in summer),* is on the principal shopping street Calle Larga. You can download an information package to your mobile phone here.

Background

Possibly founded by the Phoenicians, Jerez was an unimportant Roman town called Ceret; what is known is that wine was produced here even back in those times. The Moors took the city, which they named Sherish, after an epic battle in which they defeated a Visigothic army 10 times larger than their own force. It was reconquered in 1251 by Fernando III but subsequently lost in 1264; the commander of the Christian garrison, García Gómez Carillo, so impressed the Moorish victors that they spared his life and set him free. They may have regretted this, for he promptly assembled a force and advanced on the town, taking it back after a five-month siege. The borders of the emirate of Granada lay just to the east, earning Jerez its surname 'de la Frontera' (of the frontier), which it shares with many other towns in this area.

Jerez was already famous for its sherry in 15th-century Britain and the tipple has been popular there ever since, whenever the two countries haven't been at war. Barons is an appropriate word for the heads of the sherry-producing families, who have traditionally treated the town as a private fiefdom. Many of the *bodegas* are at least partly British in origin, and the town's upper classes today still appear to be a curious hybrid of the two countries. In contrast, Jerez also has a large and close-knit gypsy community, many still living in the old town of Barrio de Santiago, and is a real centre of flamenco.

Places in Jerez de la Frontera

The centre of Jerez is the elegant **Plaza del Arenal**, whose southern end is full of tables of poor-quality tourist restaurants. Many of the city's principal sights and several of its best tapas bars are within a short distance of here.

The **Alcázar complex** ① *Alameda Vieja s/n, T956-326923, Mon-Sat 1000-1730, Sun 1000-1430 winter, Mon-Sat 1000-2000, Sun 1000-1500 summer, €3; €5.40 including a camera obscura that has shows every 30 mins until 30 mins before closing*, has a bit of everything. A sturdy fortress built by the Almohads, it was a sometime residence of Sevillan kings

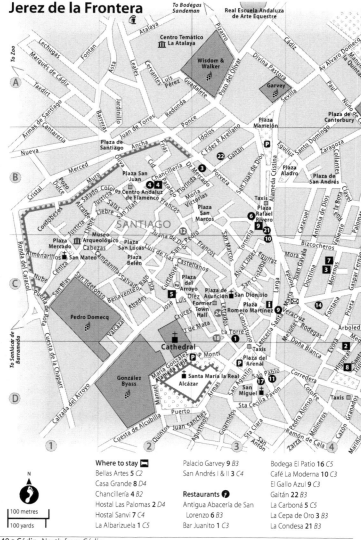

Jerez de la Frontera

Where to stay 🛏	Palacio Garvey **9** B3	Bodega El Patio **16** C5
Bellas Artes **5** C2	San Andrés I & II **3** C4	Café La Moderna **10** C3
Casa Grande **8** D4		El Gallo Azul **9** C3
Chancillería **4** B2	Restaurants 🍴	Gaitán **22** B3
Hostal Las Palomas **2** D4	Antigua Abacería de San	La Carboná **5** C5
Hostal Sanvi **7** C4	Lorenzo **6** B3	La Cepa de Oro **3** B3
La Albarizuela **1** C5	Bar Juanito **1** C3	La Condesa **21** B3

of that era. It preserves some atmospheric Arab baths as well as the interesting church of Santa María la Real, which retains many features from its days as a mosque, including the *mihrab*. The Palacio de Villavicencio is a mostly 18th-century structure that houses a camera obscura giving views over the city and as far as the coast. The Alcázar's gardens are particularly well maintained and try to lend a Moorish ambience.

Just opposite the Alcázar complex, Jerez's **cathedral** ① *Mon-Sat 1100-1300, 1830-2000, Sun 1100-1300, free*, is built over the site of the former main mosque. There are high stained-glass windows of saints along the central nave and a fine Zurbarán Madonna and Child, but little else of great artistic merit.

The **Iglesia de San Miguel** is the most interesting of Jerez's churches. Situated a short way south of Plaza del Arenal, it is immediately noticeable for its ornate 17th-century bell tower, which unusually stands right above the middle of the main entrance, a surprising, ornate, geometrically decorated facade dating from the same period. Around to the left is the original main door, an Isabelline portal with elaborate Gothic pinnacles. Inside, the main *retablo* is a masterpiece by Juan Martínez Montañés.

Near the cathedral, the **Plaza de Asunción** is a beautiful square with two proud buildings on it: one is the 15th-century church of San Dionisio with yet another *mudéjar* belltower, while the other is the former town hall, with a superbly carved Platesresque facade and curious loggia with two rows of arches.

North of here stretch the narrow streets of the oldest part of the town, part of which is the *barrio* of Santiago. One of the curious things about Jerez is that alongside its well-heeled sherry population is a large gypsy community whose flamenco almost rivals the wine in quality and fame. Santiago is still the centre of the gypsy population and is a good spot for a wander, with several interesting churches and a couple of museums. Of the former, San Mateo is worth a visit primarily for its staggeringly elaborate Baroque *retablo*. The *barrio* used to have an authentic, seedy charm, but recent renovations and modern apartments have removed some of its character.

Museo Arqueológico

ⓘ *Plaza Mercado s/n, T956-333316.*
Although not a patch on the excellent museum in Cádiz, Jerez's archaeological museum is very attractive, with its collection laid out around a light patio as well as darker, atmospherically lit chambers. It was closed for refurbishment at the last update.

Centro Andaluz de Flamenco

ⓘ *Plaza San Juan 1, T856-814132, www.centroandaluzdeflamenco.es. Mon-Fri 1000-1400.*
This important centre holds a large archive of printed music, recordings and videos of flamenco; it's Spain's main body for the promotion of the art. As well as temporary exhibitions, screenings of performances by some of the flamenco's greatest names are shown daily; you can also request videos from the archive. The centre is free to enter and is also a good source of information about upcoming events and performances.

Jerez Zoo

ⓘ *C Taxdirt s/n, T956-182397, www.zoobotanicojerez.com. Tue-Sun 1000-1800 (daily 1000-1900 summer). €6 3-13 year olds, €9 adults.*
A kilometre or so beyond the Barrio de Santiago is the city's zoo, with animals housed in a peaceful botanic garden. Although, as usual, you find yourself wishing the animals had more space, the organization does its best, and the creatures seem well cared for; there's also a centre for treating sick and wounded animals found in the wild. All in all, it's one of the country's best. The big draw here is a rare white tiger, named Kyosu.

Real Escuela Andaluza de Arte Ecuestre

ⓘ *Av Duque de Abrantes s/n, T956-318008, www.realescuela.org. The show takes place every Tue and Thu at midday, also on Fri in Aug. On weekdays when there's no show, complete visits 1100-1400. Show €18, complete visit €10. Reserve in advance by phone or via the website.*
This training centre for the white Carthusian horses (see box, page 39) is a popular attraction. In the show the elegant dancing beasts sashay around to symphony music, with riders dressed in traditional costume. Dubbed an equestrian ballet, it really is quite astounding. When there's no show, you can watch the training sessions; it's very enjoyable to watch horse and rider develop the necessarily close relationship required to perform such complex movements; at these times you can also visit the stables, palace, and two museums – one of equestrian art, one of carriages.

Centro Temático La Atalaya

ⓘ *C Cervantes 3, www.elmisteriodejerez.org. Entry in groups by time slot. Tue-Sat 1000-1500, 1800-2000, Sun 1000-1500. Admission to Palacio del Tiempo/Misterio/both €6/5/9.*
This much-hyped complex combines two museums. Jerez's much-loved collection of clocks and watches has been given a contemporary slant and renamed the **Palacio del Tiempo** (Palace of Time). It's an absorbing collection of pieces from all over the world that now takes the form of a voyage through time. Next to it is the newly opened **Misterio de Jerez**, a museum devoted to the sherry industry, with numerous fancy special effects.

Bodegas

Most of sherry's big names have their *bodegas* here: Domecq, González Byass, Sandeman, Garvey and many more. Most of the *bodegas* can be visited, although many require a phone call the day before. This is worth the effort (everyone in the Jerez wine trade seems to speak good English) and rarely a problem; if you're lucky you'll get a very personal tour.

Of sherry and other Andalucían nobles

James Bond: Pity about your liver, sir. Unusually fine Solera. '51, I believe.
M: There is no year for sherry, 007.
Diamonds Are Forever.

Sherry wines are produced in the area around Jerez de la Frontera, from which their English name derives. The region has a long winemaking history; the wines of Jerez were popular in Britain long before Shakespeare wrote about Falstaff putting away quarts of 'sack' to drown his sorrows or keep out the cold. Britain is still the biggest consumer and there's a distinctly British air to the area's winemaking culture.

The two principal grapes used for the production of sherry wines are the white *Palomino Fino* (the majority) and *Pedro Ximénez*. The region's soils have a massive influence on the final product; the chalky *albariza* tends to produce the finest grapes. Palomino produces the best dry wines, while Pedro Ximénez tends to be dried in the sun before pressing, optimizing its sugar levels for a sweeter wine.

There are two principal styles of sherry, but no decision is taken on which will be produced from each cask's contents until a couple of months after the vintage. This decision is taken by the *capataz* (head cellarperson), who tastes the wines, which are poured using the distinctive long-handled *venencia*, designed so as not to disturb the yeast on the wine's surface. Those that will become rich, nutty *olorosos* are fortified to about 18% to prevent yeast growth; these wines are destined for ageing and may later be sweetened and coloured to produce styles such as cream or *amoroso*. The best *olorosos* may be aged 25 years or more. *Finos*, on the other hand, are fortified to a lower level and nurtured so as to try and optimize the growth of the naturally occurring local yeast, *flor*. This produces a pale, dry wine, with a very distinctive clean finish, perfect with seafood tapas.

Manzanillas are *finos* that have been aged in the seaside environment of Sanlúcar de Barrameda; the salty tang is perceptible. Half a million litres of *manzanilla* is drunk during the Sevilla Feria alone, and *manzanilla* sales account for more than half of sales of dry sherry in Spain. At around 15 degrees of alcohol, it's the lightest of the sherries. *Amontillados* are *finos* aged longer than normal so that some oxidation occurs after the protective layer of yeast has died away. Some of these are sweetened for the British market.

Another curiosity of sherry production is the use of the *solera*. This is a system of connected barrels designed to ensure the wine produced is consistent from one year to the next. The wine is bottled from the oldest barrels (butts), which are in turn refilled from the next oldest, until the last are filled with the new wine. While the wine produced has no vintage date, the age of the *solera* is a matter of pride, and there are many around that are well over a century old. The butts can be used for up to 100 years.

Another similar Andalucían wine is *Montilla*, from Córdoba province. Much like a sherry in style, the difference lies in the fact that they are rarely fortified. Málaga wines are fortified and mainly sweet; those from the highest grade, *lágrima*, are pressed using only the weight of the grapes and can be very good.

Brandy is also made in Jerez. Although connoisseurs of French brandies usually sniff at the oaky nature of these coñacs, there are some good ones produced, and even the cheaper varieties are rarely bad. The spirit is produced using sherry casks, and the same *solera* system is employed.

The two most-visited *bodegas* don't require a booking and are handily near the cathedral. The most famous sherry is **Tío Pepe**, the second-level *fino* produced by **González Byass** ① *C Manuel María González 12, T956-357016, www.bodegastiopepe.com, hourly tours in English and in Spanish, daily tours in German, €11, or €16 for the 1400 visit which throws in some tapas*, the biggest of Jerez's producers. Their massive complex can be visited on a slick, slightly Disneyfied tour. You'll learn nothing about the sherry-making process but will have a pleasant ride around the pretty *bodega* in a small train. Highlights include a pavilion designed by Gustave Eiffel, drunken mice, barrels signed by all manner of celebrities who have visited, and a tasting room left in original early 19th-century state. Although the tour is pricey, there's a generous tasting session at the end of it. Book online at busy periods.

Just up the hill from the cathedral, **Pedro Domecq** ① *C San Ildefonso 3, T956-151500, www.bodegasfundadorpedrodomecq.com, Mon-Fri 1000-1300, Sat 1200, €8, children under 16 free*, is a good *bodega* to visit. The tour is more informative and personal than González Byass. Staff will happily give explanations in English alongside the Spanish. The tour takes in both the sherry and brandy ageing areas, and has a glass-ended barrel so you can see the thick *flor* yeast. There are signed barrels here too, including one by Franco. When King Alfonso XIII visited the *bodega*, the Domecq family considered it a discourtesy to make him cross a public street to get from one part of the complex to another. The solution: they bought the street, a typical piece of sherry baron thinking. The tasting here is exceptionally generous – you'll want to have had a decent breakfast – and includes two brandies, one of which, **Fundador**, was Hemingway's standard tipple when in Spain.

The tourist office has a list of other *bodegas*. One of the smaller but worthwhile ones is **Sandeman** ① *C Pizarro 10, T956-151711, www.sandeman.es, Mon, Wed and Fri 1100-1430, Tue and Thu 1015-1500, €7*, who do a good tour, with plenty of English tours. You can pay more for an enlarged tasting with better wines.

Around Jerez de La Frontera

Ten kilometres from the city on the way to Medina Sidonia, **La Cartuja** ① *Ctra Jerez-Medina Km 9, T956-156465, gardens open Mon-Sat 0930-1115, 1245-1830*, a beautiful Carthusian monastery, is still occupied by a community of the white-robed monks. It was here that the *cartujano* breed of horse was developed and refined (see box, page 39). It's well worth dropping by to admire the harmonious Baroque facade and take a stroll in the gardens. Zurbarán's superb series of paintings for the monastery church can now be seen in the Cádiz museum.

One of the most important Carthusian horse studs, **Yeguada de La Cartuja** ① *Ctra Medina Sidonia-El Portal Km 6.5, T956-162809, www.yeguadacartuja.com, every Sat at 1100, €10*, is located off the road between Medina Sidonia and El Portal, a few kilometres beyond the La Cartuja monastery. There's a weekly tour of the stables including a show and various runnings; it's advisable to reserve this in advance.

North from Cádiz listings

For sleeping and eating price codes and other relevant information, see pages 11-15.

⊘ Where to stay

El Puerto de Santa María *p33, map p34*
Its excellent transport connections mean that El Puerto makes a good base for the Carnaval at Cádiz; there are also festivities going on here. While it's easier to bag a room here than in Cádiz, you'll still need to book well in advance.

€€€€ Hotel Monasterio San Miguel, C Larga 27, T956-540440, www.hotelesjale. com. One of the more luxurious spots around and a place where the king himself has laid his head, this former monastery is now a large and comfortable hotel with a rainforest garden, swimming pool, top restaurant and antique furniture. Rooms are large, but at this price you might want to pay the extra and get a suite, which are particularly comfy.

€€€ Casa de los Leones, C La Placilla 2, T956 875 277, www.casadelosleones.com. A beautifully renovated 18th-century house next to the food market, this place holds exhibitions and is named for the creatures atop the pillars either side of the front door. The house is centred around a patio; the galleries are exquisite, with chessboard tiling, wooden ceilings and wrought-iron balustrades. The accommodation is in spacious apartments with dining table, kitchen, microwave, fridge, and washing machine; they have 1 or 2 double bedrooms and are remarkably cheap (**€€**) off season.

€€€ Hotel Los Cántaros, C Curva 6, T956-540240, www.hotelloscantaros.com. Just behind the seafood strip, this attractive and hospitable hotel has bright and cheery rooms decorated in differing styles. Once a prison, it couldn't have changed more. Staff are usually excellent. Prices drop significantly off season. Parking available.

€€ Hotel Casa del Regidor, Ribera del Río 30, T956-877333, www.hotelcasadelregidor.

com. Set around a sweetly restored patio, this 2-star hotel offers value, compact rooms with free Wi-Fi and a most affable welcome right in the heart of El Puerto's eat street. That means there's a fair bit of noise in the front rooms at weekends and in summer.

€ Hostal Esperanza, C Jesús de los Milagros 21, T956-873593. Right in the thick of things, this 3-room spot compensates for its slightly worn-feeling rooms with an obliging owner, rapid hot water and moderate prices. The 2 doubles are much better than the tiny single.

€ Hostal Loreto, C Ganado 17, T956-542410. This charming choice is set in a traditional old *portuense* house and is engagingly cluttered with pot plants and old furniture. All rooms have a clean bathroom; it's a good deal and handily located in the shopping area near the tourist office.

Camping

Camping Playa Las Dunas, Paseo Marítimo La Puntilla, T956-872210, www.lasdunas camping.com. A large site by the beach with excellent facilities including a pool and a party atmosphere in summer. There are also bungalows of various sizes.

Sanlúcar de Barrameda *p35, map p36*
There are few options here, and rooms are harder to find in summer.

€€€ Hotel Tartaneros, C Tartaneros 8, T956-362044, www.hoteltartaneros.net. A beautiful early 20th-century building at the head of the avenue near Plaza del Cabildo. The decor is rather staid, but the rooms are comfortable and have facilities such as minibar, safe and satellite TV. There's also a large attractive patio to have a drink or breakfast.

€€€ Posada de Palacio, C Caballeros 11, T956-365060, www.posadadepalacio.com. A cracking spot opposite the Palacio de Orléans-Borbon set in a smart 18th-century *palacio*. The house has a lovely patio and sunny terrace; the rooms (of which there are a variety) are furnished in understated belle epoque style, with charming beds, plush armchairs and balconies overlooking the garden. Recommended.

€€€-€€ Palacio de los Duques Medina Sidonia, Plaza Condes de Niebla 1, T956-360161, www.ruralduquesmedinasidonia.com. An opportunity to stay in a working palace, ducal seat of the Medina Sidonia family. There's a variety of elegant double rooms, furnished in antique style, and hung with family portraits and ducal heirlooms. The prices include breakfast in the charming café here. The money goes to fund the late duchess's cultural foundation.

€€ Hotel Barrameda, C Ancha 10, T956-385878, www.hotelbarrameda.com. An oasis right off the main street in the heart of town, this hotel is built around a pretty patio and decorated with photos of the Doñana wetlands. Rooms are cool, with marble floors and comfortable beds. You pay about €10 extra to get a room overlooking the pedestrian street; a little noisier, but worth it to feel part of the town. There's free Wi-Fi, and a scorching roof terrace gives a chance to take the sun. Recommended.

€ Hostal Blanca Paloma, Plaza de San Roque 9, T956-363644. Handy central *pensión* overlooking this busy square. Rooms are basic but comfortable, equipped with fan and washbasin; the shared bathrooms are clean. Good value even in summer.

€ Pensión La Bohemia, C Don Claudio 1, T956-369599. Lovely budget accommodation near the Iglesia de Santo Domingo. The place absolutely gleams, so thoroughly are its pretty *azulejos* scrubbed; the rooms are cosy and have good, if small, modern bathrooms. Recommended.

Jerez de la Frontera *p38, map p40*

€€€ Hotel La Albarizuela, C Honsario 6, T956-346686, www.hotelalbarizuela.com.

Stylish modern small hotel, all clouded glass, stencilled lettering, and white minimalism, recalling the chalky *albariza* sherry soil for which the hotel is named. The rooms are very clean and attractive, the bathrooms good and the staff friendly.

€€€ Hotel Palacio Garvey, C Tornería 24, T956-326700, www.sferahoteles.net. This small hotel is set in a striking neoclassical sherry baron's mansion on Plaza Rafael Rivero and makes an excellent base in the centre. The rooms offer 4-star comfort and are decorated in a modern black and white style that's attractive but seems a little at odds with the noble building, which includes an elegant patio-lounge. Service is excellent, and the hotel is very good value in summer (**€€**). Recommended.

€€ Hotel Bellas Artes, Plaza del Arroyo 45, T956-348430, www.hotelbellasartes.com. Opposite the cathedral, this is an elegant but friendly spot set in a beautiful 18th-century house. Its walls are soothing pastel colours and thoughtfully decorated with paintings, including some imaginative woodcut prints in the chambers. The rooms are very attractive, and all a little different. It's worth nabbing one on the street if you can, as they're much lighter. Some have stone vaulting, while others feature old-style bathtubs. The suites (**€€€**) come with a jacuzzi. There's a fantastic roof terrace looking right at the cathedral. Prices include a good breakfast.

€€ Hotel Casa Grande, Plaza de las Angustias 3, T956-345070, www.casa grande.com.es. Excellent value is on offer at this central hotel in an elegantly converted art deco mansion, with cool marble-floored rooms taking the sting out of the Jerez sun. Extra features like an elegant library lounge and spacious roof terrace mean you're not confined to quarters, and the staff are approachable and helpful.

€€ Hotel Chancillería, C Chancillería 21, T956-301038, www.hotelchancilleria.com. Secreted away in the heart of Barrio de Santiago, this newish hotel has a romantic flamenco-land location and backs it up with excellent service and inviting rooms with a/c, Wi-Fi, and great firm beds. It's been designed in an eco-friendly manner and offers a grassy patio, sunny terrace and recommendable restaurant. Recommended.

€ Hostal Las Palomas, C Higueras 17, T956-343773, www.hostal-las-palomas.com. Likeable budget option with rooms around a nice light patio on a quiet street. It's well run, and they're good value for money, being attractively furnished and spacious; some are better than others so ask to see a couple. There are a couple with shared bathroom, but the price difference is only €5.

€ Hostal Sanvi, C Morenos 10, T956-345624. Run by a friendly family, this is a very likeable option on a quiet street not far from C Larga. The rooms are small but colourful and have modern bathrooms. They have no exterior windows but open on to the airy central corridor. A bargain *hostal*, with parking available for €6 per day. Recommended.

€ San Andrés I & II, C Morenos 12, T956-340983, www.hotelsanandres.es. This is a 2-in-1 place, a *hostal* and hotel. Both have beautiful patios full of tropical plants and attractive rooms, some with balconies, the hotel's with modern bathroom and both with heating. There are a few rooms without bathroom available but the prices are similar. Friendly owners.

Street MICAELA ARAMBURU CASTIGAS NEAR TOURIST OUR

Restaurants

El Puerto de Santa María p33, map p34
El Puerto is a very inviting place to eat. The Ribera de Marísco near the ferry dock has a string of restaurants. There are some excellent tapas bars in the parallel street Ribera del Río and its continuation Misericordia, behind it. It's popular to duck across on the boat from Cádiz for a boozy lunch.

€€€ Aponiente, C Puerto Escondido 6, T956-851870, www.aponiente.com. The avant-garde cuisine on offer at this central gastronomic highlight may be at odds with El Puerto's conservative core, but remains very much rooted in local tradition, for the chef creates all sorts of new flavours with sherry and the yeast used to produce it. Correct service is complemented by smart contemporary design.

€€€ El Faro de El Puerto, Ctra Fuentebravía Km 0.5, T956-858003, www.elfaro delpuerto.com. Established by the same owners as **El Faro** in Cádiz (see page 28), this elegant mansion and gardens just outside town showcases the finest of Spanish seafood in refreshingly different ways. You might want to try the black rice with squid and cuttlefish, a lighter dish of red mullet with aubergine, or the utterly sensuous *carabineros* in oloroso sherry. The service is faultless and wine list good.

€€ La Taberna del Puerto, C Ribera del Río s/n. Just along from the Ribera del Marisco is this likeable stone place with its wood beams and barrels of good *manzanilla* and moscatel. At weekends it's very popular, when there's an in-house seafood stall and folk happily munching away on tasty fare.

€ La Antigua, C Misericordia 8, T687-797709. Offering an upbeat welcome and tasty vacuum-poured Rioja and Ribera wines in case you've tired of sherry, this convivial place has tasty seafood meatballs and *ensaladilla* with prawns among its various offerings.

€ La Bodeguilla del Bar Jamón, C Misericordia 5, T956-850322. Another reliable option, this bar is at its busiest on Sun, when, at precisely 1430, the star tapa is unveiled: a delicious seafood rice. Be there promptly, as it has a tragically short lifespan as the hungry hordes tuck in. At other times, there's good *berza* (pork and vegetable stew) and big *panes* (open sandwiches). Photos of frighteningly large pigs overlook proceedings.

€ Mesón del Asador, C Misericordia 2, T956-540327. With a more populist feel than some of the smarter bars around here, this spacious and cheery locale draws you in with the aromas of grilling meats. Tasty pork and beef tapas might have you moving to a table for a bigger serving.

Chipiona *p35*

There are many eating options, including a few bars within the port itself.

€€€ **Paco**, T956-374664. Closed Tue and Nov. This is a place for a serious seafood meal; the chef buys his fish direct from the boats outside so it is fresh as can be. Prices are fair (but ask to avoid nasty surprises), and the quality is sky high; you can also come here for tapas. Recommended.

Sanlúcar de Barrameda *p35, map p36*

The best spot is Bajo de Guía, where a row of seafood restaurants with terraces looking over the river cater to every budget.

€€€ **Casa Bigote**, Bajo de Guía s/n, T956-362696, www.restaurantecasabigote. com. Closed Sun and Nov. The *sanluqueño* restaurant with the most formidable reputation. It maintains very high standards and a meal on the terrace by the beach won't be forgotten in a hurry, unless you overindulge on the *manzanilla*. There's efficient service and a fine range of fresh seafood. House specialities include *langostinos* (king prawns) and *raya* (skate). They also run an excellent tapas bar a few doors up. Recommended.

€€ **Cantina**, C Infanta Beatriz 2, T956-360742. Despite being part of an ugly hotel and Guinness-free 'Irish' pub complex, this tapas bar manages to rise above its station. At tables in an attractive low wine cellar you can enjoy fine *raciones* and very generous tapas. The *solomillo* is excellent – you can have it with a variety of sauces – and there's also seafood on offer. For a rich treat, you can't, however, beat quail stuffed with *foie*.

€€ **Casa Balbino**, Plaza del Cabildo 11, T956-360513. One of the province's most memorable tapas stops, this main square option is a must, even if you have to use force to get to the bar. The friendly staff will have your *manzanilla* on the bar before you've even asked; the wide range of tapas are excellent, including tasty stuffed potatoes and *tortillita de camarones*. The whole town stops here for a tapa before lunch, and the atmosphere is great; it's an experience just watching bar staff in action. There's an outside terrace too (but no table service). Highly recommended.

€€ **La Lonja**, Av Bajo de Guía 8, T956-383642. Another reliable seafood terrace overlooking the beach and the water. Try 200 g of *navajas* (razor shells) washed down with *manzanilla*, then tackle a seafood rice for 2 while enjoying the sunshine.

€ **Bar Juanito**, Plaza San Roque s/n, T956-368137. A friendly bar with a small terrace on this interesting square. The tapas are superb, including several types of prawns, sea snails, and tasty *ensaladilla*. Around midday, it's full of locals grumbling about football and politics.

€ **Bodegas la Cigarrera**, Plaza Madre de Dios s/n, T956-381285. This atmospheric old wine *bodega* has an equally charismatic bar and patio area to enjoy a glass of their delicious *manzanilla en rama* and typical tapas.

€ **Despacho de Vinos Las Palomas**, Plaza de Abastos, T956-368488. Occupying the ground floor of a fine old mansion, this bar has a beautiful wooden ceiling and a sizeable bull's head watching over proceedings. You'll almost feel guilty paying only €0.70 for a glass of local *manzanilla*, which comes with olives; other tapas are mostly tasty *montaditos* and preserved fish snacks.

€ **La Taberna Taurina**, C Santa Ana s/n. A few steps from the main pedestrian street but a world away, this place offers a glimpse of a rapidly disappearing side of Spain, with men, *manzanilla*, bulls, football, and no frills.

Cafés

Heladería Bornay, Plaza del Cabildo s/n, T956-877742. This café and ice cream parlour is a Sanlúcar institution and over a century old. Now with many branches around town, this is still the best spot to sit on the terrace right in the heart of the action.

Jerez de la Frontera *p38, map p40*

The town boasts some excellent restaurants and tapas bars; many of the dishes use sherry, which is also often drunk here as an accompaniment to a meal.

€€€€ La Condesa, Plaza Rafael Rivero, T956-326700. The restaurant of the **Palacio Garvey** hotel, this can also be entered up an alleyway off C Larga. It's an atmospheric spot that has developed a high reputation. The decor is modern but comfortable, with bright red chairs, and the classy cuisine offers decent value and plenty of innovation, but doesn't always hit the heights the ambience might suggest. There's a *menú de degustación* for €40.

€€€ La Mesa Redonda, C Manuel de la Quintana 3, T956-340069, www.restaurante mesaredonda.com. An established and traditional Jerez restaurant which is deservedly popular. Local cuisine includes, of course, tasty meat dishes in some sort of sherry sauce. If it's on, try the seriously delicious *caldereta* stew.

€€€ Tendido 6, C Circo 10, T956-344835, www.tendido6.com. Closed Sun. Despite the garish neon sign, this is a classy restaurant. With a location opposite the bullring, there's no prizes for guessing the main theme of the decor, but it's a warm, comfortable spot with fine service. The meat is good, but there's also excellent fish, such as *urta*, a popular local variety of bream. There's also a tapas bar attached.

€€ Bar Juanito, C Pescadería Vieja 4, T956-334838. One of Jerez's classics, this is a place that must be visited during your stay. With a small bar, large covered patio for dining, and a beautiful terrace shaded by white cloth, it's a welcoming spot, and the quality of the food is excellent. Ask the bar staff what they recommend; suggestions include *carrillada*, artichokes, prawns, *berza*, or calamari, washed down with a selection from a long list of sherries.

€€ Bodega El Patio, C San Francisco de Paula 7, T956-340736. There's something very Jerez about eating in a converted sherry warehouse, and this place is one of a few that fits the bill. With plenty of atmosphere, and reliable local cuisine, you might as well stick to staples like kidneys cooked in, you guessed it, sherry. There's a worthwhile lunch menu.

€€ El Gallo Azul, C Larga 2, T956-326148. Right in the heart of things, this fine tapas bar and café is set in an unmistakeable round brick building dating from the early 1900s which used to be a famous meeting place for Jerez intellectuals. There's a good restaurant on the 1st floor, but the greatest pleasure here is to have a *fino* in its narrow bar or on the terrace, and pick from some of the fine cold seafood canapés at the counter.

€€ La Carboná, C San Francisco de Paula s/n, T956-347475. A cavernous restaurant set in an old sherry *bodega* offering polite service, plenty of space, and, thanks to the high ceiling, a quieter dining experience than in many Spanish restaurants. There's everything from quail to giant *chuletón* steaks here and you're generally better off on the meaty side of things. There's a €30 menu matched with sherries and tapas at the bar.

€€ La Cepa de Oro, C Porvera 35, T956-344175. A cosy place popular with all sorts of people and open for years. The homestyle cooking is the big attraction; this is the sort of spot to try classic Andalucían dishes such as *berza* (a spicy stew of beans, sausage and cumin) or *rabo de toro* (bull's tail). There's a small terrace on the lively street. Service can be on the gruff side, particularly if the Xerez football team are on a bad run.

€€ Las Banderillas, C Caballeros 12, T956-350597. Originally decorated, with breeders' marks on the walls and several clever touches, this bar is decked out like a little *plaza de toros*. The chunky darts that it's named after are everywhere, as are photos of them being stuck into bulls. The icy *fino* is a relief on a typical Jerez summer's day, and the delicious tapas are served with a smile.

€€ Restaurante Gaitán, C Gaitán 3, T956-345859. A Jerez classic for traditional cuisine, this is a great spot. The inviting dining room is all arches, small tables, pictures and pot plants. The restaurant does the heavy things best, like bull's tail and steaks, and also has a decent wine list. There's a 4-course menu matched with different sherries.

€€ Sabores, C Chancillería 21, T956-301038, www.restaurantesabores.es. Romantically situated in Barrio de Santiago, the restaurant of the Chancillería hotel is a modern but atmospheric small place offering excellent fresh produce from a short, quality menu. There's a little garden area that makes for great dining on a warm evening.

€ Antigua Abacería de San Lorenzo, Plaza Rafael Rivero s/n. There's a handful of popular ham 'n' cheese tapas bars on this small square. This has a terrace with big tables and a lively scene. The deli-style tapas are tasty, and the sherry glasses sizeable.

€ Café La Moderna, C Larga 65. As down to earth as you can get in central Jerez, this popular bar/café is always lively and has an excellent atmosphere. The back room is lovely, with wooden beams and brick vaulting up against a fragment of the old city walls. There are also simple filling tapas available, such as stews of beef, venison or tripe (*menudo*). The beer is cheap, too.

€ Tabanco San Pablo, C San Pablo 12, T956-338436. An authentic bar, where the sherry barrels are not for decoration but consumption. It's an old-fashioned Spanish spot with yellowing bullfight posters on the walls; the sherry is served in humble glasses and doesn't taste any the worse for it. There's not a big range of food, but the *montaditos* are sensational, especially the ones with *chorizo*. Recommended.

€ Vinoteca Jerezana, C Arcos 6, T956-320288. This is a no-frills bar to buy decent *fino*, or knock one back rubbing shoulders with wise old locals. The prices and atmosphere confirm you've taken the exit ramp from the touristy part of sherrytown.

🍷 Bars and clubs

El Puerto de Santa María *p33, map p34*
There are several bars in the streets behind the Ribera de Marísco, as well as the floating **La Pontona** on the water, but in summer head to Playa de Valdelagrana, which is one long raucous strip of nightlife, with *chiringuitos*, pubs, and *discotecas* galore. The in places change every summer, so just head down and see where it's all happening.
Bahía de Cádiz This popular casino is 5 km outside of town, on the road to Jerez.
El Loco de la Ribera, Plaza de las Galeras Reales 3, www.locodelaribera.com, is a curious and rather charming bar opposite the ferry port. It draws all sorts, and has regular live music. It's definitely worth a stop.

Sanlúcar de Barrameda *p35, map p36*
The best zone for bars is the grid of streets around Carril San Diego and C Santa Ana. There are several *discobares* around here.
Bajo de Guía 67, Bajo de Guía 67, T956-367143. With low terrace chairs outside by the beach at the end of this seafood strip, this makes a good place to relax after a shellfish meal. Inside are art exhibitions, thoughtfully selected music, and eclectic concerts every Fri.

Jerez de la Frontera *p38, map p40*
Jerez generally has a quiet nightlife and it can be difficult to find a busy bar midweek. The main nightlife area at weekends is along Av de Méjico, which has a range of bars. C Divina Pastora has a few bars, while on C Zaragoza are a couple of decent *discotecas* and the Plaza de Canterbury, a lively summer square with a few bars around it. There are also a couple of options near Plaza Asunción, but the proximity of El Puerto de Santa María, with its booming summer nightlife, means people are used to heading over there for a big night out.
Don Juan, C Letrados 2, T956-343591. Open 2100-0100. You couldn't get much more Jerez than this elegant little bar. It

attracts a dressy young to middle-aged set for quiet drinks and chat.
Duplicado, Plaza Vargas 2, T956-326329. A beautifully decorated bar, done out in wood and brick with hanging musical instruments. There's a friendly mixed bohemian clientele.

⊙ Entertainment

Jerez de la Frontera *p38, map p40*
Flamenco
Jerez is an important centre of flamenco and you can find both the touristy dinner and dance packages as well as classy performances in smoky bars. The best place to find out about upcoming performances is the Centro Andaluz de Flamenco (see page 42); the newspaper *Jerez Información* also has a flamenco page.

There are many *peñas* and flamenco bars; some of the most authentic include:
Café El Arriate, C Francos 41. The photos on the wall commemorate some of the greats of Jerez flamenco, and there are scheduled and spontaneous performances.
El Lagá de Tío Parrilla, Plaza del Mercado s/n, T956-338334. Closed Sun. Although there are plenty of tourists, the flamenco here is often of very high quality. Daily shows at 2230 and 0030; entry free, but drink prices are steeper than normal.
La Bulería, C Mariñíguez 15, T956-323468. Another likely spot to find something good at the weekend.

⊙ Festivals

Sanlúcar de Barrameda *p35, map p36*
Sanlúcar has a notable Semana Santa, with processions through the old town.
End of May The Feria de la Manzanilla is a dressy occasion similar to the Feria of Sevilla. It celebrates the town's winemaking tradition by consuming as much as possible of it. The Whitsun pilgrimage to El Rocío is also a busy time here, as many of the brotherhoods gather in Bajo de Guía to be ferried across the river.

Aug Horse races (see page 37).
13-15 Aug Fiesta, where the local Virgin is carried through the streets in procession over colourful patterns made from dyed salt crystals.

Jerez de la Frontera *p38, map p40*
Feb/Mar Festival de Flamenco. Check dates at www.festivaldejerez.es.
Easter Jerez's Semana Santa processions are similar to Sevilla's and worth seeing.
First half of May The Feria del Caballo, Jerez's main fiesta, runs for a week. It's quite similar to Sevilla's Feria de Abril, but has a more serious horsey aspect, and there are more public *casetas*. It's also when the city's best bullfights are scheduled and often coincides with the motorcycle grand prix, which fills the city to bursting point at any time. There are other horse events, either racing, or dressage, throughout the year.
9 Oct The celebration of San Dionisio, the town's patron saint.

⊙ What to do

Sanlúcar de Barrameda *p35, map p36*
The Real Fernando is a chunky old boat that runs trips from Sanlúcar across to the Coto Doñana. These depart daily at 1000; and also at 1600 (Mar, Apr, May, Oct) and 1700 (Jun-Sep). The trip takes 3½ hrs and includes 2 stops. You can rent binoculars on board (€3). It's essential to reserve a place as far in advance as you can (T956-363813, www.visitasdonana.com). The boats leave from opposite the building and the trip costs €15, €7.50 for 5-12 year-olds. Commentary is also in English.

The 4WD tours of the park from El Acebuche sometimes pick up people who have booked from Sanlúcar; they get ferried across by a launch. Book well in advance, T959-448711.

Jerez de la Frontera *p38, map p40*
10 km east of Jerez is its Circuito Permanente de Velocidad, www.circuito

dejerez.com. This racing track has hosted the Spanish Formula 1 Grand Prix, and is the established venue for the motorcycling Grand Prix. All year there are other motor-racing events here at weekends.

⊖ Transport

El Puerto de Santa María *p33, map p34*
The tourist office keeps an up-to-date timetable of departures.

Boat A catamaran service goes to **Cádiz** 5-10 times daily, 30 mins, €2.20 each way.

Bus There are buses to **Cádiz** every 30 mins or so (40 mins), leaving from the square outside the bullring. From the same spot are regular departures for **Sanlúcar** and **Chipiona**, while from near the train station, buses also go to **Jerez** hourly or more.

Train El Puerto is on the Cádiz-Jerez *cercanía* line and there are frequent services in each direction. There are departures every 30 mins or less, taking 12 mins to **Jerez** and 35 mins to **Cádiz**. **Sevilla** is also frequently served (1 hr 20 mins), via **Lebrija** and **Utrera**.

Sanlúcar de Barrameda *p35, map p36*
Linesur goes from the station on Av de la Estación. Hourly buses go to **Jerez** (30 mins) on weekdays; every 2 hrs at weekends. 11 daily buses (5 at weekends) run to **Cádiz** (1 hr) via **El Puerto de Santa María**. There are also hourly departures to **Chipiona** (15 mins), and **Sevilla** (2 hrs).

Jerez de la Frontera *p38, map p40*
Jerez's bus and train stations are close together in the east of town. The city is especially well connected with Sevilla and Cádiz. Frequent local buses (No 10) run to and from Plaza del Arenal in the centre, or it's about a 15-min walk.

Air Jerez's airport is 8 km northeast of town off the Sevilla road. It has a daily Ryanair

service to and from **London** Stansted as well as **Frankfurt** Hahn, **Madrid** and **Barcelona**. Various other German and European destinations are served by charter airlines.

Bus Local: There are buses every 30 mins to **Cádiz** (40 mins), hourly or more often to **El Puerto de Santa María**, and buses hourly to **Sanlúcar de Barrameda** (30 mins). Going east, hourly buses go to **Arcos de la Frontera** (40 mins), via **Ubrique**. 11 buses daily go to **Algeciras**, 3 of these go via **Tarifa**, some going on to **La Línea**, at the Gibraltar border. 4 buses go to **Conil** daily. **Long distance**: Linesur runs buses to **Sevilla** (1 hr 15 mins), with 11 weekday departures and 7 at weekends.
  There are 4 daily buses to **Ronda** (3 hrs, via **Arcos de la Frontera**), 1 to **Málaga** (5 hrs), 1 to **Granada** (5 hrs), and 1 to **Córdoba** (except Sat).

Car rental ATESA, Aeropuerto de Jerez, T956-150014, www.atesa.es. One of a few agencies at Jerez airport.

Train Jerez is on the main Sevilla-Cádiz train
line. There are *cercanía* departures every 30 mins or less to **Cádiz**, taking 50 mins via **El Puerto de Santa María** (12 mins). **Sevilla** is also frequently served (13 or so a day, 1 hr 5 mins), via **Lebrija** and **Utrera**.

⊙ Directory

Jerez de la Frontera *p38, map p40*
Language schools Linguae Mundi, C Enrique Rivero 18, T956-349696, www.linguae-mundi.com. **Medical services** For medical emergencies, go to the Hospital General, Ctra de Circunvalacion s/n, T956-032000. For non-emergencies go to the central **Centro de Salud**, C José Luis Díez 14, T956-033665. **Post** Jerez's main post office is on C Cerrón 2, T956-342295.

White towns of Cádiz

East of Jerez, and stretching into Málaga province, the famous white towns of Andalucía preserve much of their original Moorish street plan and are spectacular, whether viewed from afar, perched atop their steep hills, or from up close, lost in their webs of narrow, winding streets. But they are far from being quaint little villages; they were important Moorish and Christian cities and strongholds, the homes of dukes and nobles who have left them with a stunning architectural legacy of palaces and churches. Arcos is the most visited and has an impressive collection of characterful accommodation.

Arcos de la Frontera → *For listings, see pages 61-64.*

One of the most striking of the white towns, and the most westerly of the series that runs into Málaga province, Arcos has a dramatic position on a hilltop, with many buildings worriedly peering over the edge of the crumbly cliffs. Approaching from Jerez, you won't get this viewpoint; it's worth taking the Avenida Duque de Arcos that runs along the bottom of the cliff for the best view. Arcos has an ancient history, having been founded by the Romans as Arco Briga; it was expanded by the Moors and even became the seat of its own little *taifa* kingdom. It held out against the Reconquest until 1264; it can't have been the easiest spot on earth to conquer.

Arcos' **tourist office** ⓘ *T956-702264, turismo@ayuntamientoarcos.org, www.arcosdela frontera.es, Mon-Fri 1000-1430, 1600-1900, Sat 1030-1330, 1600-1800 (1700-2000 summer), Sun 1030-1330; guided tours of the town (€3) in Spanish, Mon-Fri 1030, 1200, 1700, 1830, Sat 1030, 1200,* is in the old town, on the central Plaza del Cabildo.

Places in Arcos de la Frontera
While the new town sprawls unattractively from the main road, the older part is a perfectly preserved network of narrow streets, with a North African feeling of white buildings studded with the sandstone facades of *palacios* and churches. From the new town, the main street, Calle Corredera, climbs along the ridge of the hill up to the heart of the *casco antiguo*, the Plaza del Cabildo, which has a mirador with fine views.

Opposite stands the **Basílica de Santa María** ⓘ *Mon-Fri 1000-1300, 1530-1830, Sat 1000-1400, €1.50, closed Jan and Feb*, whose buttresses you had to pass under while ascending the street. The Baroque belfry looks a bit curious tacked on to what is essentially a late Gothic church. It's surprisingly small inside, but you can admire the high panelled golden *retablo* topped by Plateresque stonework. It seems a pity that for some reason the congregation face the other way these days. The sacristy has a fine frieze and ceiling; but it's the exterior west facade that is the real masterpiece, an Isabelline Gothic work with very ornate piers decorated with niches and pinnacles.

On the west side of Plaza del Cabildo the castle looms. While it was once the Moorish stronghold, it owes its current appearance to the 15th century. Unfortunately, today it's a private residence and not open to the public.

From here, wander to your heart's content through the narrow streets to the east. There are several *palacios*, with delicately carved facades, and another interesting church, **San Pedro** ① *Mon-Sat 1000-1300, 1600-1900, Sun 1000-1330, €1*, which has a fine Baroque bell tower and another excellent painted *retablo*.

Following a lane around the back of San Pedro, the street leads downhill to another fine mirador with 270-degree views over the fertile *vega* below town and the artificial lake that gives citizens relief from the summer heat.

Medina Sidonia

This ancient white town was originally settled by the Phoenicians. The Romans fortified the hilltop and called the colony Asido Caesarina; it later became an important Visigothic and Moorish town. It was recaptured under Guzmán El Bueno, the hero of the defence of Tarifa; the town and lands were granted to him and he thus became the first duke of Medina Sidonia. This aristocratic line has been Spain's most powerful and, for centuries, the dukes were the country's largest private landowners. Medina Sidonia is less touristy than other white towns and only 35 km from Jerez.

The town has preserved a rich array of remnants from its various ruling civilizations. Dominating the small walled precinct at the top of the hill is the church of **Santa María la Mayor la Coronada** ① *daily 1030-1400, 1600-1830, €1*. It preserves the courtyard of the original mosque; the mossy bell tower was once its minaret. The staggering *retablo* dominates the Gothic interior, a memorable 16th-century work with five rows of panels depicting the life of Christ painted and sculpted by Juan Bautista Vásquez and Melchor Turín. There's a fine sculpted Christ by Pedro Roldán.

Opposite the church is a small **information office** ① *T956-412404, daily 1000-1400, 1600-1800 (on Sat mornings it operates from a kiosk on Plaza España)*. Plaza España, the long and elegant main square, has terraced cafés and the Ayuntamiento at one end.

Other things to look out for while wandering around town are the restored 10th-century horseshoe entrance gate, the **Arco de la Pastora**, and lofty vaulted Roman sewers. The castle is poorly preserved.

Off the A396 a couple of kilometres east of Medina Sidonia, **Acampo Abierto** ① *T956-304312, visits mid-Mar to mid-Oct Wed, Fri, Sat 1130, €18*, is a bull-breeding ranch which puts on a show (in several languages) of those beasts as well as horse riding.

Parque Natural Sierra de Grazalema → *For listings, see pages 61-64.*

East of Arcos, the *pueblos blancos* (white towns) continue. Some are situated in one of Andalucía's best walking regions, the Parque Natural Sierra de Grazalema. Although it's one of Spain's wettest areas, the rain is seasonal and means that a great variety of vegetation, including many pine species, can flourish in the limestone formations. The attractive villages of El Bosque and Grazalema make the best bases for hiking; both offering lots of accommodation and hearty mountain food. There are many other places to explore: north of these villages is the enchanting hamlet of Zahara de la Sierra and beyond that, the marvellously atmospheric towns of Olvera and Setenil de las Bodegas; the other way is the leather-working town of Ubrique; while, further south en route to the coast, the castles of Jimena and Castellar beckon.

El Bosque

Simply named 'the forest' like a place in a fairytale, El Bosque is indeed completely surrounded by trees, mostly pines. It's the gateway to the Parque Natural de Sierra de Grazalema and an important stop for prospective walkers, as you need to get a permit for hiking in most of the park, which is restricted for environmental reasons. It's a notable trout-fishing village; even if you don't fancy casting a fly, you can enjoy other peoples' fishing efforts in the local restaurants. El Bosque is also a centre for hanggliders; there's a popular launch spot in the hills above the town. Otherwise, it doesn't make the most appealing base of the towns in the area.

The main information centre for the natural park is the **Centro de Visitantes** ① *Av de la Diputación s/n, T956-727029, www.egmasa.es, daily 1000-1400, plus Fri and Sat 1600-1800 (Oct-Mar) or 1800-2000 (Apr-Sep)*. It's on a small square just below the main road. Regulations for park entry change frequently and there are various restricted areas. Permits are free, but should be arranged as far in advance as possible as there are daily quotas for various parts of the park. You can arrange them in person or over the phone.

East of El Bosque, the small village of **Benamahoma** is a peaceful place, also accessible on foot along the river in about an hour.

Grazalema

Hard facts come first in serious guidebooks and it has to be said that Grazalema receives more rainfall than any other spot in Spain. It's a remarkable microclimate, as villages as little as 5 km away receive barely a quarter of the precipitation. Don't be put off, however, as the rain comes down mainly in November, April and May; at other times there's a sporting chance of good weather. Grazalema is one of the prettiest of the *pueblos blancos* and is the major base for walking in the park (see below), with accommodation and eating options to reward a hiker on any budget. The rain, in fact, contributes to the area's appeal, as it's the lushness of the vegetation that makes it such a pleasant spot for rambling about. Although now mostly reliant on tourism, there are still important blanket-making and carpentry industries, just as in the days when the British sociologist Pitt-Rivers wrote his famous study of the town, *People of the Sierra*.

Founded by the Romans, and then expanded by the Moors, it was not reconquered until very late in the day, in 1485. There are four churches in town; the **Iglesia Parroquial** is the most impressive, a 17th-century Baroque work. Wandering around the streets is a pleasure, peering into craft workshops as you go. One of them, on the main road to Ronda, contains a small **museum** ① *Mon-Fri 0800-1400, 1500-1830*, on the rug trade.

The town's **tourist office** ① *Plaza de España 11, T956-132225, Tue-Sun 1000-1400, 1600-1800 (1700-2000 Apr-Oct)*, on the central square, is really more of a shop and tour agency, but it is able to provide limited information and can arrange permits for walking in the park.

Practicalities and walking The Parque Natural Sierra de Grazalema is an area of some 500 sq km that has been declared a UNESCO Biosphere Reserve. It's a great haven for birds, including the golden eagle and Egyptian vulture, and huge colonies of the more common griffon vulture. It also sees many migratory species en route to and from the Straits of Gibraltar. Among its lush vegetation is a concentration of *pinsapo*, an increasingly rare variety of native fir. The terrain is extraordinarily varied, with jagged formations of karst giving way to poplar-lined valleys and thick stands of cork and evergreen oaks alternating with olive and almond groves and with wheat and barley fields.

Permits While you can walk in most areas of the park, certain zones require a permit to walk through them. This includes the zone northwest of Grazalema, roughly extending to Benamahoma and Zahara de la Sierra. Permits can be arranged through the visitor centre in El Bosque (see above), but can usually be organized by telephone (you'll need an email address and access to a printer), or via the tourist offices in Grazalema or Zahara de la Sierra. As daily numbers entering the park are restricted, try to arrange your permit as far in advance as possible.

Due to the restrictions imposed on walking, the well-marked paths are fairly sparsely hiked; you may well meet nobody on a day out in the hills here. You should obtain the good 1:50,000 map of the area, published by the Junta de Andalucía/Instituto Geográfico Nacional, and stocked by all the tourist offices in the zone.

Grazalema to Benaocáz via El Salto del Cabrero → *Distance: 11-14.5 km. Time: 4-4½ hrs or 5½-6 hrs. Difficulty: medium (short route), medium–difficult (long route). At the time of writing, no permit required, but check this situation.*

This is one of the Sierra's most beautiful walks. There are constant changes of terrain, great views to the west across the rolling countryside that leads down towards Jerez and on clear days to the Atlantic. You'll have a steep climb first thing if you leave from Grazalema (longer route) but you can avoid this by taking a taxi up to the Puerto del Boyar (call Rafael at the **Casa de las Piedras**, T617-315765). Due to its popularity this walk is best undertaken on a weekday. Get going by 0930 to allow time for stops and a picnic along the way and to make the 1540 bus from Benaocáz back to Grazalema (Monday-Saturday). You could have lunch in Benaocáz. Beautiful stands of ancient oaks, interesting karst formations, exceptional flora and raptor-spotting possibilities make this a varied trip. **Map**: 1:50,000 Parque Natural Sierra de Grazalema or 1:50,000 Series L 1050 Ubrique.

Longer route Leave Grazalema's square by passing between the **Unicaja** bank and the Ayuntamiento along Calle José María Jiménez. Bear left at the end past **Bar La Cabaña**, climb to the top of Calle Real then turn into Calle Portal. Take the next right and continue climbing to the top of the village where you should bear left past the Fromental cheese factory and then turn right on to the Grazalema–El Bosque/Zahara road. Just before a bridge turn left off the road then follow a new path up through the pine trees all the way to the top of El Puerto del Boyar (50 minutes). Here pick up the itinerary below.

Shorter route Take a taxi to the parking area at the top of the pass between Grazalema and El Bosque, El Puerto del Boyar. Just behind a sign for 'Peligro de Incendio' go through the wire-and-post gate to the left of a second larger gate then follow a track gently downwards. Just before reaching a farm (20 minutes) bear left, away from the track, towards two old oaks where dogs may be tethered. Go through a wire-and-post gate and head across a large, flat area past some magnificent old oaks. At the far end the path crosses a tumbledown wall then winds through thicker undergrowth, at times dividing. Keep left at any fork, sticking close to the cliff. The path soon swings sharply right, drops down by a wall, passes through a graffiti-covered gate, then descends. Be careful not to drop too far to your right; if in doubt, keep left at any fork, staying fairly close to the base of the cliff. The path eventually leads through another gate (50 minutes) where a walker symbol marks your way. After the gate bear right and climb to a flatter area; a lovely spot for a first break. The path now passes to the left of a fallen oak then climbs up through the brambles before reaching a large field. Head for the water trough at the bottom of the field then bear left and climb, following the same line as that of the trough. An indistinct path loops to the top of this open area then arcs right past a fallen oak (ignore a path which bears left and crosses a tumbledown wall). The path bears left to a wall and reaches a gate. Go through and continue, roughly parallel to the wall before angling right across open, rocky land towards the back of El Salto del Cabrero, or the Goatherd's Leap, whose grey massif is now directly ahead. Look for clumps of peonies between the rocks. Near the bottom of this rocky descent you climb over a wall then break out on to a vast, flat area (one hour, 40 minutes) at the eastern base of the Salto. You emerge by a clump of oaks where there is welcome shade: a great spot for a picnic. It's possible to scramble up to the top of the Salto from here. A lot of the climb is hands-on, there's no clear path and you should allow an hour to get up and down. Otherwise you should bear left, away from the Salto across this vast open area.

At its far side you pick up a path that crosses a wall before climbing gently across another open tract of land. The path soon levels and Benaocáz comes into view. You'll shortly see a farm ahead of you which you should leave well to your left. The path soon descends, passes to the right of an old lime kiln then zigzags down through the rocks to a gate (two hours, 15 minutes). You may spot griffon vultures perching on the cliff face to your right; look for their tell-tale guano. After the gate the path (loose underfoot) loops down to a flatter area then runs along beside a hawthorn-topped wall, passes through a green gate then follows the old drover's path whose ancient cobbling is still visible in parts. After crossing a stream by way of a pretty bridge it swings right, climbs, then widens to become a track which soon passes by some ugly, modern housing then the **Hostal San Antón**. At a garish villa bear left to the centre of Benaocáz (three hours) where **Bar La Palmera** is the best place to slake your thirst. Later head down Calle San Blas (by the Caja de San Fernando) and take the first left to reach the bus stop. The bus passes by at 1540, arriving at Grazalema 20 minutes later.

Benamahoma to Zahara de la Sierra → Distance: 14 km. Time: 6-6½ hrs. Difficulty: medium-difficult. Permit required.

If you don't mind walking along tracks rather than paths this makes for a truly great full-day excursion. The hardest part comes first thing, a long pull up from 500 m to 925 m via a well-surfaced track that hugs the course of the Breña del Agua stream. There are great views of the Sierra del Pinar and the Sierra del Labradillo. The second half of the walk is nearly all downhill with views eastwards into the gorges of Garganta Seca and Garganta Verde, home to one of Europe's largest colonies of griffon vultures. You'll almost certainly see several dozen of these enormous raptors during the walk. Steel yourself for a steep final haul up to Zahara. This route links two of the Sierra's prettier villages; if staying overnight, Zahara is recommended. The predominance of track rather than path means that you can forget where your feet are going and concentrate on the amazing views.

Take plenty of water. You'll need to take a taxi to the beginning or end of the walk. This is easily arranged in Zahara (Diego: T956-123109) or Benamahoma (Horacio: T956-716199). **Map**: 1:50,000 Parque Natural Sierra de Grazalema or 1:50,000 1050 Ubrique and 1036 Olvera.

Route The walk begins at the bottom of Benamahoma at the bus stop, next to **Venta El Bujío**. From here walk away from the village and take the first right turn at a sign for 'Molino de Benamahoma'. Cross the river and after some 40 m, where the road swings right, turn left. Follow a fence along for 50 m then swing right and climb straight up between two fences on a rough track to a white sign. Here turn right and go through a large, rusting gate. Ignore a left fork just after the gate and stick to the main track; prepare yourself for nearly 1½ hours of climbing. The track goes through a metal gate (45 minutes) and 10 minutes later swings right past a ruined farmstead then arcs to the left. Shortly you reach a goat pen and drinking troughs to the left of the track. Careful! At the first large oak to the left of the track after the troughs look for a small cairn. Here bear left away from the track (one hour, 15 minutes) following a path which climbs, indistinctly at first, to the top of a small pass (one hour, 30 minutes) where it divides. Take the left fork and drop down between the oaks. As you descend, looking ahead, you'll see a gently convex hillside. Head for its left side and soon you'll spot the track that you will later follow, cutting down across it. Sticking to this same course, a building with a white-posted gate comes into view. Head for it keeping the Sierra Margarita to your left. You reach a gate which may be locked but you can go through a second smaller gate to its left. Soon to your right you'll see the Laguna del Perezoso, a shallow watering hole which is often dry. The track reaches a farm where it arcs right and a well-surfaced forestry track leads you down through lovely stands of ilex oaks overgrown with hawthorn, wild olive, ivy and gorse. You go through a wire-and-post gate (two hours, five minutes) and continue your descent. Eventually the track bears sharp right then zigzags down to the valley floor where it swings left and crosses a (dry) stream. Shortly you go through another wire-and-post gate then climb through old groves of olives to the pass of El Puerto de la Breña (two hours, 55 minutes) where you break out into the next valley.

Ahead of you now are the rocky crags of Garganta Seca and Garganta Verde. Once over the pass the track bears left and descends, passing through another wire-and-post gate. Follow the main track down, ignoring tracks branching right or left. Eventually you go through a green gate (three hours, 25 minutes) and continue your descent. The track crosses the Bocaleones stream, bears left and climbs through the olive groves. Prepare yourself for today's second steep haul. You reach a pretty farm to the left of the track with a palm tree. Here, just before reaching a green gate, turn right away from the track and follow a path steeply up through the olives. You cross a (dry) stream. The path improves and continues to climb then meets with a steep concrete track that leads up towards a pylon. You pass behind a row of modern houses then turn left and almost immediately sharp right and head up a street with a no-entry sign. The road bears left and you reach a wider street that swings right then left. Follow this street and you will reach the main square of Zahara (four hours, 15 minutes).

Other walks
El Pinsapar The classic Grazalema itinerary takes you through the heart of the Pinsapo forest. This full-day excursion begins on the road leading from Grazalema to Zahara. After a stiff climb of nearly 300 m a broad path leads through a large stand of *pinsapos*. You need a permit. Start early to avoid school parties and other groups.

Other routes around Grazalema There are two waymarked routes – both half days – which begin near the campsite on the road above the village. A good and easy-to-follow day's walk is to follow the river Campobuche (sometimes called the Gaduares) to Montejaque and then return by taxi. It is also easy to follow the route from Grazalema to Zahara that drops down the Gaidovar valley, skirts round Monte Prieto to Arroyomolinos where a track begins, leading you near to Zahara.

While the A372 heads east from Grazalema straight into Málaga province, there's a little corner of Cádiz that you can explore on your way to Ronda by taking the road north to Zahara de la Sierra, and continuing in a loop round through Olvera and Setenil de las Bodegas. Zahara is reached by a road just west of Grazalema, which climbs north over the austere Puerto de las Palomas mountain pass.

Guy Hunter-Watts's *Walking in Andalucía* (Santana Books) has details of more walks in the area.

Zahara de la Sierra

Zahara is a heart-winning white village crouching under the rock that bears its much-modified Moorish castle. It's spectacular and steep even by white village standards. Below is a large reservoir. The **Iglesia de Santa María** in town is a curious mixture of the Baroque and the neo-Gothic, with an impressive gilt *retablo* inside. It makes another pleasant walking base.

There's an **information office** ① *Plaza del Rey 3, T956-123114, daily 0900-1400, 1600-1900*, which can arrange permits for the Parque Natural and has a display on the local wildlife.

There's plenty to do in the surrounding area, and **Zahara Catur** ① *T657-926394, www. zaharacatur.com*, in association with the visitor centre, organizes many activities, from canoeing and caving to guided walks.

The most interesting walk from the town is the restricted **Sendero de la Garganta Verde**, starting 3 km from Zahara up the road to Grazalema. Within minutes of leaving the car park you enter a pristine, almost prehistoric, valley with no sign of human interference except the odd sign requesting silence in a breeding area for griffon vultures or giving information about nearby rock formations. After about 30 minutes of gentle walking the path descends rapidly, passing a cliff where you can see vultures nesting (during the summer, access to this area may be prohibited by the park authorities), into a canyon with sheer rock faces rising above, up to 400 m in some areas. The air becomes cooler as you follow the old river bed filled with huge boulders and unusual rock formations and descend deeper into the canyon. The route becomes slightly more hazardous at this point as you are required to clamber over rocks to a large cave called the Cueva de la Pileta. It is well worth the effort; the cave is made of an unusual pink rock with stalagmites and stalactites and is some 30 m high and approximately 75 m wide. Rock climbing equipment and a special permit are required to continue beyond this point as the route along the canyon becomes increasingly steep. The return journey is almost entirely uphill. Allow approximately four to five hours from the road for a round trip; only 30 people are allowed access at any one time.

Olvera

In the northeast corner of Cádiz province, and rising high above the surrounding countryside, Olvera is visually dramatic from the moment you espy it. The church looms over the town, and, even higher, its Moorish castle is improbably perched on a small crag. Olvera is an olive-growing town and offers majestic views over the surrounding hills, dappled with trees. It was reconquered by Alfonso XI in 1327 (his first triumph), and was on the frontline until 1482, when most of the sierra towns that remained in Nasrid hands began to fall.

The beige twin-towered church, **Nuestra Señora de la Encarnación**, dominates the plaza at the top of town. Here, by the entrance gate to the fortress, is a helpful **tourist office** ① *T956-120816, Tue-Sun 1030-1400, 1600-1800, 1900 in summer*. They sell tickets (€2) for the castle and a good museum on 14th-century life. There's also an interesting map showing the castles in Andalucía (in Spanish only).

Olvera is also a starting point for a *vía verde*, a disused railway turned into a trail for walkers and cyclists. This heads 36 km to Puerto Serrano through tunnels and over viaducts. The tourist office can provide a map.

Setenil de las Bodegas

One of Andalucía's most intriguing villages, Setenil is set on the sinuous Río Trejo on the edge of Cádiz province near Ronda. The river has carved a ravine, and many of Setenil's houses are dug into caves, hence the town's name. Many are overhung by the brooding rock above; in some places the overhang is so great that it covers both sides of the street.

There's a 15th-century late Gothic church and the ruins of a Moorish castle, but admiring the extraordinary houses is the real attraction here.

There's an exceedingly helpful **tourist office** ① *in a shop above the central Plaza de Andalucía, C Villa 2, T659-546626, www.setenil.com, Tue-Sun 1000-1400, 1700-2000*. You can arrange guided visits and activities in the region here.

Instead of heading east to Ronda, you may want to drop down to the coast at Algeciras via the impressive white towns of Ubrique, Jimena and Castellar.

Ubrique

South of El Bosque, this busy town is attractively set in a valley under steep limestone crags. It's famous in Spain for being one of the doughtiest Republican towns during the Civil War; its never-say-die guerrillas took to the hills despite overwhelming odds and defied the Nationalist armies for some time. These days it is equally renowned as the home town of bullfighter Jesulín. It's also noted for its leatherwork. Most of the action is in the new town, but the old part is atmospheric for a stroll.

The town was once a Roman settlement, and there are a few remains on the edge of town. Ruins of the Moorish castle, **El Castillo de Fátima**, are located 3 km away.

The town's helpful **tourist office** ① *C Moreno de Mora 19, T956-464900, turismo@ sierradeubrique.com*, can arrange a visit to one of the leather factories.

Jimena de la Frontera

South of Ubrique, this is another prettily located white village topped by the remains of a Moorish castle. It was a significant Roman town, Oba, which minted its own coinage. Many prehistoric sites have also been found in the immediate vicinity, including the important cave paintings at **Laja Alta**. These Bronze Age artworks depict a variety of stick figures in different positions and, interestingly, ships, the only known depiction of sailing vessels from this period.

Jimena is on the eastern edge of the **Parque Natural Los Alcornocales**, a thickly wooded region of hills and cork trees that is one of Andalucía's largest natural parks. Between the hills are a series of *canutos*, narrow valleys supporting a range of tropical and subtropical ferns and shrubs. The many limestone caverns support an important bat population; it's thought that 18 of the 26 species present in the Iberian Peninsula hang out here. Wild boar, deer, otters and both Egyptian and griffon vultures are also about. The tourist office here can provide a list of walks in the region.

Jimena's **tourist information point** ① *T956-640569, Mon and Wed-Fri 1100-1400, 1600-1800, Sat and Sun 1100-1400*, is located below the castle at the top of the village.

The castle itself stands on the brow of the hill, looking over the town on one side and the cork forests on the other. It's open at all hours to wander around, but preserves little besides its flowerpot-like keep and a fabulous triple-arched entrance gateway. The inspiring view extends to the Rock of Gibraltar.

Castellar de la Frontera

There are actually two towns bearing this name, a legacy of a curious piece of social history. The original, and the one of interest, lies 8 km west of the main road. As the place was so isolated and decayed, Franco's government built the inhabitants a new home on the main road. The original village was repopulated by mostly German artists and hippies; this caused plenty of conflict once the original inhabitants started drifting back to claim houses that the immigrants had saved, an oft-repeated scenario with abandoned villages throughout Spain.

The old Castellar is a remarkable village that's actually contained within the protective walls of its castle, which is in an utterly dominant position. It's wonderfully atmospheric, with cobbled streets, and little whitewashed houses with window boxes. From the battlements of the castle, you get fabulous views to Gibraltar and Morocco. Many of the houses are *casas rurales* (see page 63). There's an information centre below the castle. There are several art and craft workshops worth a look.

There are no buses to Castellar de la Frontera; you have to get off an Algeciras–Jimena bus (see page 64) at the new Castellar and walk or hitch (neither are bad options) the 8 km to the village.

White towns of Cádiz listings

For sleeping and eating price codes and other relevant information, see pages 11-15.

🛏 Where to stay

Arcos de la Frontera *p53*

Arcos has many worthwhile places to stay, including several *casas rurales* in town and the surrounding region. Email the tourist office for a list.

€€€ Parador Casa del Corregidor, Plaza del Cabildo s/n, T956-700500, www.parador.es. Right on the main square with fabulous views out from the clifftop, this smart hotel is located in a typical Andalucían mansion, slightly severe from the outside, but with beautiful interior patios. All the rooms are comfortable, but try to get one with views over the *vega* rather than the square.

€€ Hotel El Convento, C Maldonado 2, T956-702333, www.hotelelconvento.es. A beautifully restored old monastery in the heart of the village, with very hospitable owners. The rooms are elegant and well looked after, with modern bathrooms and a/c; those with a terrace cost more, but they're all good value. Recommended.

€€ La Casa Grande, C Maldonado 10, T956-703 930, www.lacasagrande.net. A tiny, individual hotel with only 4 rooms in a pretty-as-a-picture mansion in the centre of the old town. There are charming doubles and a couple of suites, all decorated with a personal Andalucían touch; the beds have big fluffy pillows and,

for a tropical touch, mosquito nets. The roof terrace is the highlight, staring right at San Pedro church. Recommended.

€ Hostal San Marcos, C Marqués de Torresoto 6, T956-700721. A small and quiet *pensión* with a charming roof terrace and light, clean rooms with a/c and bathroom at a very good price. There's also a washing machine for guests' use. Recommended.

Camping

Camping Lago de Arcos, Santiscal s/n, T956-708333, www.campinglagodearcos. com. A well-equipped campsite by the lake below the town, open all year and with a pool, shop and restaurant.

Medina Sidonia *p54*

€€ Hotel Medina Sidonia, Plaza Llanete de Herederos s/n, T956-794092, www. tugasa.com. A hotel on a quiet street near the church that is set in an elegantly converted *palacio* with an attractive whitewashed patio. The rooms are light on the eye and pleasant. Good value.

€ Hostal Amalia, Plaza de España 6, T956-410035. A very likeable cheapie on the main square. The doubles have bathroom and some overlook the plaza.

El Bosque *p55*

€€ Hotel Enrique Calvillo, Av de la Diputación 5, T956-716105, www.hotel enriquecalvillo.com. Just across the bridge from the visitor centre, this is a likeable, rustic choice with smallish but well-priced rooms that have bathroom, TV and, crucially, heating; there are also cheap meals available.

€€ Hotel Las Truchas, Av de la Diputación s/n, T956-716061, www.tugasa. com. The classiest sleeping option in town, it's a smallish hotel by the river and much favoured by anglers in trout season. The rooms are comfortable if a little like a chain hotel in style; the best have balconies. The restaurant is cosier, with a fireplace and, of course, trout featuring large on the menu. There's also a pool.

€ Albergue Juvenil El Bosque, C Molino de Enmedio s/n, T956-716212, www. inturjoven.com. An excellent modern youth hostel situated 1 km above the main road; there's a pool and comfortable accommodation mostly in double and triple rooms.

Camping

Camping La Torrecilla, Ctra El Bosque-Ubrique s/n, T956-716095, www.campingla torrecilla.com. A pleasant site 1 km south of town on the road to Ubrique. It's open Feb-Nov. They've also got various cabins (€40-60), either with or without kitchen.

Grazalema *p55*

€€ Casa de las Piedras, C Las Piedras 32, T956-132014, www.casadelaspiedras. net. This is a great option in a welcoming white house just off the main square. It's remarkably friendly, and has spruce heated rooms around a courtyard. There's also a cosy lounge with a log fire, and a good restaurant. There are also simple rooms without bath (**€**), and the owners have apartments for rental. Recommended.

€€ Hotel Fuerte Grazalema, Ctra A-372, Km 53, T902-343410, www.fuerte hoteles. com. This cosy hotel is in the heart of the Parque Natural, and boasts spectacular views of the Sierra and the village of Grazalema, which is 5 km or a 25-min walk away. Facilities are excellent; you can hire bikes, or just admire the view from the sizeable pool. Rates include breakfast.

Zahara de la Sierra *p59*

There are several places to stay, including *casas rurales*.

€€ El Almendral, Ctra Setenil-Puerto del Monte s/n, T956-134029. Just outside the village, this place has a garden, good rooms, and an out-of-the-way, relaxing feel.

€€ Hostal Marqués de Zahara, C San Juan 3, T956-123061, www.marquesde zahara.com. Of several accommodation options, this is by far the most charismatic, set in a restored 16th-century mansion. The rooms are equipped with TV and bathroom and are heated; you pay a little more for a room with a balcony. There's also free Wi-Fi throughout and a small cave-like restaurant (dinners only; vegetarian meals available). Horse trekking and guided walks can be arranged.

Olvera *p59*

€€ Hotel Sierra y Cal, Av Remedios 4, T956-130303, www.tugasa.com. Tucked away off the main road at the eastern end of town, this is the best of Olvera's 4 lodging options. It has attractive, good-value rooms and a swimming pool. Most of the best places to eat are nearby too.

Setenil de las Bodegas *p59*

There's no accommodation in the centre.

Ubrique *p60*

€€ Hotel Ocurris, Av Solís Pascual 51, T956-463939, www.hotelocurris.com. A modern hotel named after the old Roman town. It's a comfortable choice but the owners naughtily have chosen a colour other than white to paint their building, a rebel streak that doesn't affect the hospitable service. Good restaurant and a popular café/bar.

Jimena de la Frontera *p60*

Jimena and the surrounding area have some good places to stay, including many *casas rurales* to rent; the tourist office has a comprehensive list of these.

€€ Hostal El Anón, C Consuelo 36, T956-640113, www.hostalanon.com. Beautifully restored complex of 4 joined townhouses, decorated with ceramics, and with a good restaurant. Rooms are attractive and come with heating and a/c, as well as decent bathrooms. Breakfast is included in the price, and there's a pool. Recommended.

Camping

Camping Los Alcornocales, Cruz Blanca s/n, just north of town off the A367 to Ubrique, T956-640060, www.camping losalcornocales.com. A fairly ecologically minded campsite that has good information about walking in the natural park. There is a pool, bungalows, and a restaurant. Open all year.

Castellar de la Frontera p60

In old Castellar, there are several (**€€**) *casas rurales* bookable via the **El Aljibe** restaurant, T956-236620, www.tugasa.com. They make atmospheric places to stay, as they are little village houses tucked within the castle walls.

€€ Casa Convento Almoraima, a few metres north of the turn-off to the old Castellar, T956-693002, www.laalmoraima hotel.com. Set back from the road in the woods, this excellent rural hotel, a former monastery, has elegant and relaxing rooms set around the cloister, individually decorated with attractive wooden fittings. Excellent restaurant.

❼ Restaurants

Arcos de la Frontera p53

Eating choices are limited off-season.

€€ El Convento, C Marqués de Torresoto 7, T956-703222. Run by the hotel of the same name, this lovable restaurant is set in a 17th-century *palacio* with an elegant patio to dine around. There's a wide selection of meats, including many game dishes; the *albóndigas* (meatballs) are very tasty, as is the *choco a la plancha* (grilled cuttlefish). Don't miss the *tocinillo de cielo* for dessert.

€€ La Taberna de Boabdil, Paseo de Boliches 35, T622-075102. This curious cavern offers eclectic Maghreb-inspired decor and a secluded location with views over the surrounding countryside. The spot is run with warmth and it's well worth dropping by to check it out, whether for a drink or cup of tea or the Moroccan-style dishes.

€ Hostal San Marcos, C Marqués de Torresoto s/n, T956-700721. Where the locals come in search of a midday feed, this genial old town spot offers solid homestyle cooking and a ridiculously cheap *menú del día* for €7.

€ Mesón de Lola, C Boticas 7, T956-701807. With colourful pictures on the walls and a relaxed friendly atmosphere, this is one of the town's better tapas bars. The beer is served refreshingly cold and usually comes with a free tapa. The bar does great cold potato and egg marinated *aliños*, as well as some tasty meat stews and battered prawns. Opposite is a sort of square with another bar with a great outdoor terrace for lapping up the sun.

Medina Sidonia p54

€ Paco Ortega, Plaza de España 10, T956-410157. A typical local bar, this spot opposite the Ayuntamiento is a reader-discovered gem that turns out excellent home cooking; try the crispy croquettes to see what it's all about, or go for the value-packed *menú del día*.

El Bosque p55

€€ El Tabanco, C Huelva 3, T956-716081. In the old part of town above the main road, this welcoming restaurant is spacious and dark as a good Spanish *mesón* should be. It's a fine option for trout, but there are also yummy venison stews, praiseworthy meat dishes, and paella at weekends. The bar serves great tapas and there's an attractive outdoor eating area. There are also decent rooms available (**€€**).

Grazalema p55

There are several tapas bars around the main square, in which you can try the local goat's cheese. The accommodation choices also offer good restaurants.

€€ **Cádiz El Chico**, Plaza España 8, T956-132027. A warm-hearted restaurant delighting weary walkers with its succulent roast venison, ample wine list and tasty *revueltos*. It has good service, and also caters for a wide variety of budgets; there's an inexpensive *menú del día*.

€€ **Círcúlo La Unión**, Plaza España 18, T956-132006. This good-natured social club and bar is a good option for its terrace on the square. The interior is also busy and cosy. They do fine fried fish, but you might also want to try the delicious garlicky local *butifarra* sausage.

Setenil de las Bodegas *p59*
€€ **El Mirador**, C Callejón s/n, T956-134261. Near the plaza, this offers great views over the town and sierra, and has a generous *menú del día*. They do particularly tasty rice dishes, and there's a great mixed grill for two.

❀ Festivals

Arcos de la Frontera *p53*
Easter The Holy Week processions are impressive and the floats have to be specially customized to negotiate the narrow streets. **29 Sep** Feria de San Miguel. Bulls with padded horns are let loose in the streets. The locals run before them, dodging into doorways and jumping up on street signs and balconies to evade the horns.

Zahara de la Sierra *p59*
Jun Corpus Christi festival. Streets are strewn with wreaths and bouquets of flowers.

❀ Transport

Arcos de la Frontera *p53*
There are half-hourly buses to and from **Jerez** (45 mins) on weekdays, and a few daily at weekends. There are 9 daily buses run by 2 different companies to **Cádiz** (4 at weekends, 1 hr 15 mins), and 4 to **Ronda** (2 hrs), as well as a couple to **Sevilla**. Buses leave from the station on C Los Alcaldes near the main road

to Jerez at the bottom of town. There are half-hourly buses from here up into the old town.

Medina Sidonia *p54*
There are 6-7 buses daily from **Cádiz** and hourly buses from **Jerez**.

El Bosque *p55*
There are 4 buses Mon-Fri from **Cádiz**, 2 on Sat and Sun (2 hrs) via **Arcos de la Frontera**. There are 1-2 buses on to **Benamahoma** and **Grazalema**. 6 buses run Mon-Fri from **Jerez**.

Grazalema *p55*
There are 1-2 buses from **Málaga** to Grazalema via **Ronda**; these continue to **Ubrique**.

Zahara de la Sierra *p59*
2 daily buses connect Zahara and **Ronda**.

Olvera and Setenil de las Bodegas *p59*
There's 1 bus (Mon-Fri only) from **Cádiz** to Olvera and Setenil (2½ hrs), and 2 from **Jerez**. Setenil is linked to **Ronda** 6 times daily (30 mins) Mon-Sat. You can also access Setenil by train – it's on the Granada–Algeciras line. The station is 5 km from town, so call a taxi (T956-134328).

Ubrique *p60*
There are 8 buses on weekdays from **Jerez** to Ubrique, but none at weekends. There are 4 buses from **Cádiz** on weekdays, and 2 on Sat and Sun (2 hrs 15 mins). There are 1-2 daily connections to **Grazalema**, continuing to **Ronda** and **Málaga**.

Jimena de la Frontera *p60*
There are 2 buses daily from **Algeciras** (30 mins) as well as trains, and 1-2 to **Ronda**. The RENFE station is 1 km below town; there are 4 daily trains to and from **Algeciras** (36 mins); these continue in the other direction to **Gaucín**, **Ronda** (1 hr 7 mins), **Bobadilla** (an important rail junction), **Antequera** and **Granada** (3 hrs 40 mins).

Costa de la Luz

The most enticing stretch of the Andalucían coast runs south from Cádiz to Gibraltar. It has a range of vast sandy Atlantic beaches, some calm, some with serious surf, and is happily free of much of the overdevelopment that plagues the Mediterranean coast. Backing the beaches are rolling pastures that rise to a chain of green hills. There's a variety of settlements to choose from: from the bourgeois-bohemian vibe of Los Caños de Meca to the Moorish ambience of Vejer via the windsurfers' haven of Tarifa. What attracts the sailboarders, however, is the wind, which is more or less a constant presence, from the poniente west wind to the wailing levante east wind, which howls through town like an avenging Old Testament angel. Don't despair; at least you can exfoliate and suntan at the same time. There's plenty to do away from the sand; the Roman ruins at Baelo Claudia are impressive, the castle at Tarifa was venue for one of the Reconquista's most famous acts of courage, and the alleys of Vejer are a delight to wander. One of the most exciting aspects of this coast is that you can see the mountains of Morocco looming to the south across the Straits. It's quite feasible to pop across for a day trip or longer, as Tanger is just 35 minutes on the boat from Tarifa, or 70 minutes on a ferry from the port of Algeciras.

Conil de la Frontera and El Palmar

Likeable Conil is the first place south of Cádiz really worth a stop. A sizeable fishing town with an excellent long beach, it becomes a busy but pleasant resort in summer. The **Torre de Guzmán** near the beach is the town's main monument; it is all that is left of a castle once built by Guzmán El Bueno. A recent over-restoration has converted it into an exhibition space. Opposite, the **Museo de Raíces Conileñas** displays objects from traditional Conil rural and domestic life.

Directly in front of the Paseo Marítimo is the beach of Los Bateles, usually good for families with children as it's calm and shallow. It stretches south to El Palmar – see below – and north to La Fontanilla beach, with plenty of clifftop development but a couple of fine summer *chiringuitos* and a busy seafood restaurant. North of here, the cliffs follow the curve of the bay round to the fishing port and lighthouse. Just before the port is a turning to **Cala El Aceite**, a secluded and popular cove of perfect sand. Behind the port, the tree-shaded river is a pleasant place for less blustery swimming and picnics. The town's **tourist office** ① *T956-440501*, is near the **Comes** bus stop on Calle Carretera.

The quiet little hamlet of **El Palmar**, a few kilometres south of Conil, makes a very appealing place to relax and has a fantastic windswept beach. It's popular for surfing, and several surf schools offering lessons and equipment hire back the length of the strand, particularly north of the main access road to the beach.

Los Caños de Meca and Cabo Trafalgar

A short way further south from El Palmar, the villages of Zahora and Los Caños de Meca blend into each other. Between them is a beautiful sandy cape with a lighthouse, **Cabo Trafalgar** (accent on the last syllable around here). If you've ever fed the pigeons or waited for a night bus under Nelson's column in London, it's because of what happened just off here on 21 October, 1805. A combined French and Spanish fleet were pulverized by a smaller but technically superior British force; Spanish naval power never really recovered from this devastating defeat. The victorious British commander Horatio Nelson was killed early in the engagement; his Spanish counterpart Admiral Gravina also perished, as did over 6000 men (90% of them Spanish and French) and 18 ships.

Los Caños de Meca is one of the finest beaches on this coast and is named for the cascades of water (*caños*) that pour from its low cliffs. The village was once home to a hippy community, and, although now it's also destination of choice for a smart Spanish crowd, there's still a laid-back alternative atmosphere to the place, with beach parties, Moroccan-style *jaima* tents erected and plenty of people sleeping rough under the stars. Zahora, too, has a long and inviting stretch of sandy beach.

Barbate

The road from Los Caños de Meca to Barbate climbs through sand dunes covered with umbrella pines; this zone, known as La Breña, is encompassed in a *parque natural*. Walking in these peaceful woods makes a relaxing break from life on the beach.

The road then descends to Barbate, passing a spectacular sandy beach before winding its way past the new marina. Barbate is a fishing town: even its staunchest fans (of whom there are many) wouldn't describe it as beautiful, but there's a lot of enjoyment to be had in this friendly, down-to-earth place; this is still the real Spanish seaside, and it's a working town that doesn't shut down off-season. Franco used to spend his summer holidays here – the town is still sometimes referred to as Barbate de Franco.

Barbate makes its living from tuna, and the elaborate traditional fixed nets known as *almadrabas* have changed little since Roman times. At the Barbate marina, there's an **interpretation centre** ① *T956-459804, www.atunalmadraba.com, Mon-Sat 0900-1400, free*, with information about the *almadraba* tuna fishing. From here, there are boat trips which take you out around the big *almadraba* outside of town and along the coast.

The town is famous for its tasty *salazones* (salt-cured fish preserves) such as tuna *mojama*; one of the best places to buy these tasty products is the **shop-museum** ① *Av Generalísimo 142, T956-434323*, at the entrance to town from Los Caños de Meca.

Barbate is full of good places to eat; choose one along the beachside Paseo Marítimo for sea views. As well as seafood, it is known for *churrasco*, grilled pork ribs in a hot sauce. Also worth a visit is the small **mercado de abastos**, a traditional food market.

Between the beach and the main road is the old part of town; seek out **Calle Real**, a picturesque old street that was once the heart of the community.

Vejer de la Frontera

This white town is set slightly inland and is one of the gems of this well-endowed province. Set on a high saddle-shaped hill, it's a stunning sight as you approach. The old town is still encircled by its well-preserved 15th-century walls, with gateways from the original Moorish ramparts. Vejer dates back to Roman times, but retains much of its Moorish feel, with narrow streets and glimpses of half-hidden patios. Indeed, until relatively recently, many Vejer women wore a *cobija*, a dark cloak covering the whole face but the eyes. Many scholars feel that the decisive battle between the invading Moorish forces and the Visigoths under King Roderic took place near Vejer in AD 711.

Make your first stop the helpful **tourist office** ① *Av de los Remedios 2, T956-451736, www.turismovejer.com, Mon-Sat 1000-1400, 1600-1900 (1700-2000 summer), Sun 1100-1400*, on the way up to the old town. They'll give you a map of Vejer, but ask them for the glossy brochure as well, which has more information on the sights around the place.

In the heart of the old town is the parish church, **Iglesia del Divino Salvador**. Originally built in the 14th century over the town mosque, it is in Gothic-*mudéjar* style; later additions in the 17th century used a sort of neo-Gothic style to stay faithful to the original design. Around the side of the church are part of the town walls and a gateway.

Beyond here is the castle, built by the Moors in the 9th and 10th centuries, but transformed into a 19th-century house. It preserves a horseshoe-arched portal inside the wooden door, but is currently closed to the public. Further along, you come to the Jewish quarter, with gateways in the wall giving fine views across to the new town. A local tale relates how a young couple who were architects were cemented up alive in a section of the wall here for painting their house black. At the bottom of the old town is **Plaza de España**, a pretty space with a colourful tiled fountain.

The new part of town has been sensitively designed and doesn't clash at all with the old town. There's little to see apart from a couple of fine whitewashed windmills.

On the N340 south of Vejer is the **Fundación NMAC** ① *Ctra N340 Km 42.5, T956-455134, www.fundacionnmac.com, Mon-Fri 1000-1430, 1600-1800, Sat and Sun 1000-1430 (daily 1000-1400, 1700-2030 summer), €5*, a contemporary art foundation that stages open-air exhibitions in a large wooded park. Some of the pieces are permanent, some temporary, but there are some extraordinary works usually present, and it's well worth visiting. The entrance price includes a drink in the café.

Zahara de los Atunes

This somewhat isolated town has a wild and magnificent sandy beach with big breakers. Its name means 'blossom of the tuna fish', and it is indeed by these large beasts that the town has lived for centuries. The methods of catching the tuna have changed little over the years. Shoals pass along the coast between April and June on their way to spawn in the Mediterranean, returning in July and August. The tuna, which can weigh up to 800 kg, are herded into nets where they are hooked and hauled into the boats. Much of the tuna goes to Japanese and Korean factory ships waiting off shore, but the catch has dwindled in recent years, likely due to overfishing. It's a hard industry, and Cervantes famously commented in *La Ilustre Fregona* that nobody was truly a rogue unless they had fished tuna for two seasons at Zahara.

The centre of town is likeably ordinary, although with some resort development a couple of kilometres to the south, a district someone was probably paid a lot to name Atlanterra. There's nothing to see but the superb beach apart from the ruins of the huge tuna *lonja* (market) that stands by the shore. Very quiet outside of summer, there are always a few places open to try tuna, of which there are many varieties and styles of preparation.

Bolonia and Baelo Claudia

The small village of Bolonia, on a side road populated by red long-horned cattle, is one of the coast's more alternative places, with a mixture of summer visitors giving it a great atmosphere. The beach is typical for these parts; beautiful, windswept and with clean sand. In summer, there are several places to stay and eat; off season, there's little open here apart from the interesting Roman ruins of Baelo Claudia.

Started as a settlement in the late second century BC, **Baelo Claudia** ① *T956-688530, Tue-Sat 0900-1800 (2000 summer, 1900 spring and autumn), Sun 0900-1400, free for EU citizens, €1.50 for others*, rapidly became an important Roman town for its market, proximity to North Africa and, later, for its production of salt fish and *garum*, the fish sauce that was much prized in Rome. The geographer Strabo mentions the town as being a port of embarkation for Mauritania; it was given its title of town by Claudius, after whom it is named. You enter the site via the sleek lines of the new museum, which seems too big for its own display, but has well-presented finds and information and a sweet little gift shop. Approaching the ruins, you soon realize that the town was a substantial one: it had a population of about 2000 at its peak. It had a city wall with some 40 defensive towers, and an aqueduct bringing fresh water from 8 km away. Various large villas are in the lower part of town, near the sea; here also are the remains of one of the fish processing plants. Towering over the centre of town were three temples, to Jupiter, Juno, and Minerva. Plagued by earthquakes, Baelo Claudia began to decline in the second half of the second century AD, and was eventually abandoned in the seventh century.

Apart from the Roman ruins, the pleasure of Bolonia is simply lingering on the beach. Walking south, you come to a stone circle that's a fine place to relax by the sea.

Tarifa

One of the most relaxed of Andalucían locations, Tarifa is one of the world's prime destinations for windsurfers and kitesurfers due to the almost constant winds that blow across its long, long sandy beach. A pretty town with a distinct Moorish character, Tarifa is sure to please, not least for the fact that you can nip across to Morocco for lunch on the fast ferry. In summer, the small town becomes rather congested, and it's difficult to find accommodation.

Formerly a Roman settlement, and probably a Phoenician one before that, Tarifa is named after the leader of the initial Moorish invasion of Spain, Tarif ibn Malik, who established a base here on his initial exploratory foray to the peninsula in AD 711. The fortress and town were recaptured in the late 13th century, but proved tough to retain. The town's hero is Guzmán El Bueno, a knight from León who was defending the castle against Moorish attackers. The invaders captured his son and threatened to kill him if Guzmán wouldn't yield. The knight allegedly threw down his own dagger to them, saying "I would rather have my honour and no son than my son and no honour". The boy was killed, the city held on, and Guzmán became the first duke of Medina Sidonia for his pains. A similar story occurred during the siege of the Alcázar of Toledo in the Spanish Civil War.

Tarifa's well-run **tourist office** ① *Paseo de la Alameda s/n, T956-680993, turismo@ aytotarifa.com, daily 0830-1500, summer 1000-2100*, is just outside the old town. They have lists of accommodation, tour operators, and watersports companies.

Places in Tarifa There's not a huge amount to see in Tarifa, but who'd complain when you've got 10 km of sandy beach with views of Africa thrown in for free? One of the best viewing spots is the small mirador and garden on Plazuela del Viento, a couple of blocks east of the castle. Another fine viewpoint is the **Mirador del Estrecho** a few kilometres east of Tarifa on the main road.

Tarifa's **Castillo de Guzmán El Bueno** ① *Tue-Sat 1100-1400, 1800-2000, €2*, was built in the 10th century by the Moors, partly because of significant pirate activity in the Straits of Gibraltar. After the town was reconquered by Sancho IV (who sits in sculptured majesty outside the entrance, inadvisably petting a lion), the citadel was commanded by Guzmán El Bueno (see above) and is named after him. Much of the Moorish structure remains, a bit derelict but basically sturdy; there's a foundation tablet in Arabic over one of the entrances. The keep's interior is a little bare, but used for summer concerts; there's a display on the life of Guzmán here, including various newspaper cartoons parodying his famous action. A second castle sits out on a promontory opposite and is used by the Guardia Civil.

The main church in town is the **Iglesia de San Mateo** ① *daily 0830-1300, 1730-2100; free*; whose huge block-built Baroque facade is hard to miss. The interior is more elegant in 15th-century Gothic, brightened by stained-glass windows. The sculpture of the saint

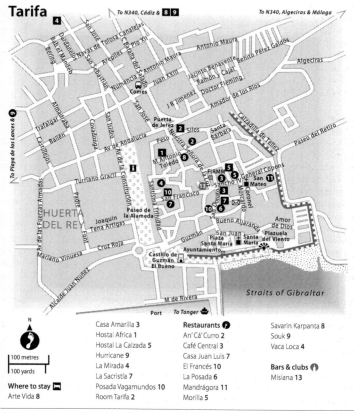

Tarifa

To N340, Cádiz & 8 9
To N340, Algeciras & Málaga

San José
Daidamia
Berlín
Bab el Mandel
Navas de Tolosa
Canalejas
San Sebastián
Arapiles
Ntra Señora de Pío XII
Antonio Maura
Antonio Maura
Jacinto Benavente
Benito Pérez Galdós
Algeciras
Numancia
San José
Juan XXIII
Ramón y Cajal
Doctor Fleming
Almadraba
Comes
J R Jiménez
Amador de los Ríos
Calzadilla de Tellez
Paseo del Retiro
Trafalgar
San Isidro
Castellejos
Covadonga
Av de Andalucía
Puerta de Jerez
Silos
Santa Bárbara
Bailén
Peso
Ntra Señora de la
FIRMM
Turriano Gracil
Santísima Trinidad
M Antonio Toledo
Sancho IV
General Copons
San Mateo
San Francisco
Coronel Moscardó
Padre
Joaquín Tena Artigas
Paseo de la Alameda
Bueno Aljaranda
Amor de Dios
HUERTA DEL REY
Cruz Roja
Guzmán
San Juan
Plaza Santa María
Santa María
Plazuela del Viento
Mariano Vinuesa
Alcalde Juan Núñez
Castillo de Guzmán El Bueno
Ayuntamiento
M de Rivera
Straits of Gibraltar
Port
To Tanger

N
100 metres
100 yards

Where to stay 🛏
Arte Vida 8
Casa Amarilla 3
Hostal Africa 1
Hostal La Calzada 5
Hurricane 9
La Mirada 4
La Sacristía 7
Posada Vagamundos 10
Room Tarifa 2

Restaurants 🍴
An' Cá' Curro 2
Café Central 3
Casa Juan Luis 7
El Francés 10
La Posada 6
Mandrágora 11
Morilla 5

Savarin Karpanta 8
Souk 9
Vaca Loca 4

Bars & clubs 🍸
Misiana 13

The coast of death

To vast numbers of North and sub-Saharan Africans, the EU is a place of marvellous opportunity: even with no papers and a menial job, a young Mauritanian or Senegalese can send much-needed money home to their family and, in a couple of years, perhaps save enough to buy a place to live back in their motherland. Little wonder then that so many set off on an arduous journey north into the unknown. Andalucía, visible from the Moroccan shore, is an obvious crossing point. Though Spain and the EU get twitchy about the numbers that make it across, a far more serious issue is the alarming number who don't.

Often paying an entire life's savings to make the journey – or more, as unscrupulous brokers often take a huge cut of any future earnings – these souls, mostly unable to swim, embark in unseaworthy vessels (known as *pateras*) into one of the narrowest, but most treacherous, stretches of water on the planet. Throw in the fact that the boatmen, to avoid capture by the Guardia Civil land patrols, often shoo their human cargo off the boat dangerously far from shore, and you have a recipe for disaster. In the last few years, thousands of bodies have been found washed up on beaches in Cádiz province; even larger numbers perhaps perish attempting the tricky crossing from Senegal to the Canary Islands.

Though coastal patrols have been upped both around Spain and in Senegal and Morocco, this seems to merely drive people to attempt the journey between points further away, exponentially increasing the danger of the crossing.

The Spanish government under Zapatero initiated reasonably humane treatment of the economic migrants who survive the crossing, and allowed large numbers to stay, despite the wrath of some other EU governments.

himself is an exquisitely rendered piece by Martínez Montañés, several of whose works adorn Sevilla's cathedral. In a side aisle is an interesting Visigothic tombstone.

At the top of the old town, the well-restored Puerta de Jerez lets you into or out of central Tarifa through its horseshoe arches. Once outside, it's worth following around to your right and turning down Calle Calzadilla, where you can admire the best-preserved section of Tarifa's imposing walls.

If you fancy a stroll, Tarifa is the start of the GR7 footpath that leads to ... Athens. If Greece seems like a bit of a hike, you can do a shorter section; the path leads through the pretty natural park of Los Alcornocales to hill villages such as Jimena de la Frontera and beyond.

Algeciras

A sizeable city, Algeciras is one of the few places in Andalucía to offer little to the visitor. The only reason to come here is to catch the ferry to Ceuta or Tanger from its busy passenger port. In summer, Algeciras is the destination for thousands of Moroccans, who head home from jobs in Europe to visit friends and family.

Algeciras has an interesting history but, unfortunately, ugly urban expansion has left almost no trace of it. It was an important Roman port, and later the landing point for the first Moorish armies in their invasion of the peninsula in AD 711. Raided by the Vikings in AD 859, it was later seized by raiding Berbers during the collapse of the Córdoba caliphate and became a self-governing *taifa* state until the rulers of Sevilla grabbed control of it. It's now one of Spain's more important ports.

The area around Plaza Alta is the best zone for a bite to eat. The **tourist office** ① *C Juan de la Cierva s/n, T956-784131, otalgeciras@andalucia.org*, is between the train station and the port; there's also a small tourist kiosk at the entrance to the ferry port area.

La Línea de la Concepción

This place, with the bay of Algeciras on one side and the Atlantic on the other, is the frontier post for Gibraltar, built after the dividing line was agreed in the 18th century; the agreement placed the town just beyond cannon range. It's a friendly town that's growing at a fast rate. If you're planning a visit to the Rock, you might consider sleeping in one of the good budget options here; unless you've a hankering for steak 'n' kidney pie, the food's generally much better this side as well. Parking your car here is also a good option for visiting Gibraltar, to avoid the border queues. There's plenty of above-ground space (but don't leave any valuables in your car); underground car parks near the border charge around €16 for 24 hours, and have deals for longer stays.

La Línea's handiest **tourist office** ① *Av Príncipe de Asturias s/n, T956-171998, www.ayto-lalinea.org, Mon-Fri 0930-1900, Sat and Sun 0930-1500*, is opposite the border post. Between here and the beach are numerous Second World War bunkers built by the Spaniards under German supervision for use in a planned attack on Gibraltar, which was codenamed *Operation Felix*. In the wake of the famous stalemate meeting between Franco and Hitler at Hendaye, this never in fact occurred. The **Museo Taurino** ① *C Mateo Inurria 2, T956-690657, Mon-Fri 1030-1400, 1700-1900*, is a likeable museum absolutely crammed with bullfighting pictures and memorabilia.

Costa de la Luz listings

For sleeping and eating price codes and other relevant information, see pages 11-15.

💿 Where to stay

Conil de la Frontera and El Palmar *p65*
Accommodation becomes pricey in Jul and Aug, but is otherwise reasonable. There are many *hostales* along C Pascual Junquera.
€€€ Hotel Almadraba, C Señores Curas 4, Conil, T956-456037, www.hotelalmadraba conil.com. This likeable small central hotel is built around a cool patio and has a roof terrace with sea views. The rooms are bright, colourful and furnished with all conveniences, including minibar and internet jack. Off-season rates are excellent value.
€€€ Hotel Fuerte Conil, Playa de la Fontanilla s/n, Conil, T902-343410, www. fuertehoteles.com. Closed Nov-mid Feb. Right on the beach, this smart hotel is set

in huge, beautiful gardens. It's very family friendly (kids stay free) and has a good pool, spa complex and a diving school. Rooms with sea view cost more, and prices are high (**€€€€**) in Aug but good value at other times. The hotel has various ecological accreditations. Prices include breakfast. Recommended.
€€ Casa Francisco, T956-232786, El Palmar. Closed Jan to mid-Mar. A great place to stay right on the beach with a fine cheap restaurant. The rooms are modern and all have sea views.
€€ Hostal La Conileña, C Arrumbadores 1, Conil, T956-444140, www.hostallaconilena. com. A good place to stay with attractive rooms that have excellent modern facilities including minibar, hydromassage bath and satellite TV. The friendly owners even screen films at night. Prices include breakfast and are cheap off season (**€**).

Camping

Camping El Palmar, T956-232161, www.campingelpalmar.es. 1 km back from the sea, with good facilities and bungalows available.

Los Caños de Meca and Cabo Trafalgar *p66*

There are many places to stay, mostly overpriced in summer and closed in winter.

€€€ Casas Karen, C Fuente del Madroño 6, T956-437067, www.casaskaren.com. Open year round, this quirky and delightful complex has a range of apartments set in characterful buildings that include a barn and thatched houses. There are hammocks to lounge about in and a very friendly owner. The apartments all have a kitchen and, while occasionally available for single-night stays, offer better value by the week. Open year round; prices almost halve off-season.

€€ El Palomar de la Breña, T956-435003, www.palomardelabrena.com. Located 6 km from Los Caños de Meca, taking the Barbate road for 3 km, and then left into the umbrella-pine forest for another 3 km. A very peaceful spot to stay in the middle of the *parque natural* dunes and excellent value outside of high summer. Also has a restaurant that specializes in chargrilled meats. Prices include breakfast. Closed Nov and only open at weekends Jan-Feb.

€€ Hostal Los Pinos, Ctra Caños de Meca A2233 Km10, Zahora, T956 437153, www.hostalospinos.com. Open year round. Opposite the campsite on the main road through Zahora, this doesn't look much from the road side. Don't be fooled; the comfortable rooms are set around an excellent pool area and the complex offers exceptional value. Laid-back, friendly service; it's a great place for a seaside break. Recommended.

€€ Hostal Mar de Frente, C Trafalgar 3, T956-437025, www.hotelmardefrente.com. Open Mar to mid-Nov. Attractive modern place at the southern end of town, beyond the Barbate turn-off at the end of the beach road. You pay more for rooms with access to the long balcony that hangs right over the beach. Other luxury rooms come with hydromassage showers.

€€ Hotel Madreselva, Av Trafalgar 102, T956-437255, www.grupocalifa.com. Open Mar-Oct. After a much-needed change of ownership and renovation, this now offers cool and peaceful seaside rooms with artfully selected furniture giving a vaguely Moorish feel. There's a pool, and breakfast is included. It's right in the centre of Los Caños.

Camping

Camping Caños de Meca, Zahora, T956-437120, www.campingcm.com. A well-equipped site open Mar-Oct, with bungalows also available. Supermarket and restaurant.

Camping Faro de Trafalgar, Av de las Acacias s/n, T956-437017. This excellent shady campsite is open year round and has a great atmosphere in summer. Has a pool, tennis courts and minigolf.

Barbate *p66*

€€ Hotel Adiafa, Av Ruiz de Alda 1, T956-454060, www.adiafahoteles.com. A few paces from Barbate's beach, this shiny newish hotel makes the best base in town. Rooms are blessed with plenty of natural Atlantic light, some, which cost a little more, have a balcony overlooking the sea. It's much cheaper off-season and they throw in continental breakfast too.

Vejer de la Frontera *p67*

€€€ Hotel Gran Sol, C Sánchez Rodríguez s/n, T956-439309, www.gransolhotel.com. Right on the beach, with burnished copper domes, this has plenty of comfort and an attractive garden area with a pool. The rooms are showing their age in parts but are comfortable, particularly those facing the sea, whose stupendous views will cost you a little more.

€€€-€€ La Casa del Califa, Plaza de España 16, T956-447730, www.lacasadel

califa.com. A bewitching spot, a warren-like place part of which was once where farmers paid their wheat tithes to the local authorities, and part of which was once an Inquisition dungeon. It's perfectly fitted in the old structure, with odd-shaped rooms decorated in quiet Moorish style. There's a variety on offer, but all have white walls, plenty of light, varnished wooden furniture, TV, phone, heating and a/c. The pricier ones have a stereo, tea-making facilities and comfy divans. There's a fabulous terrace too. Highly recommended. The same owners have a smaller hotel, No 1 Tripería (€€€; www.grupocalifa.com, same phone number), with a sumptuous patio and a pool.

€€ **Convento de San Francisco**, La Plazuela s/n, T956-451001, www.tugasa.com. Stylishly austere rooms with mod cons and antique furniture in a classily converted Franciscan monastery in the high part of town. There's a decent restaurant too, with a great tapas bar.

€€ **Hostal Buena Vista**, C Manuel Machado 4, T956-450969. Spick and span rooms with bathroom and TV in the new town; some have fine views of the village. € for most of the year.

Zahara de los Atunes p67

€€ **Hostal Marina**, C Manuel Mora s/n, T956-439009, www.donalolazahara.com. Although overpriced in high summer, this is a very good deal for the rest of the year (€). Run out of the Hotel Doña Lola at the entrance to the town, it has excellent rooms with bathroom and make a fine base for a beach stay. Great atmosphere in summer.

Camping

Camping Bahía de la Plata, Ctra Atlanterra s/n, T956-439040, www.campingbahia delaplata.com. A shady spot with plenty of trees on the beach 1.5 km south of Zahara's centre. It's open year round and can organize a variety of summer watersports. Upmarket bungalows are available for hire.

Bolonia p68

There are many places to stay and eat, nearly all closed in winter.

€€ **La Posada de Lola**, C El Lentiscal 26, T956-688536, www.hostallola.com. A beautiful choice and excellent value, this welcoming spot is soothingly decorated with cheerful colours and Asian art. The rooms are quirky and comfortable, with mosquito nets, and there's a blooming garden. There's a choice of private or shared bathroom. Recommended. Worth booking well ahead.

Tarifa p68

There is also a wide range of apartments and *casas rurales* for weekly rent in and around Tarifa; the tourist office can give you (or email) a full list.

€€€ **Hotel Arte Vida**, Ctra N340 Km 79.3, T956-685246, www.hotelartevida.com. This beautiful hotel is one of the best upmarket options on Playa de los Lances, 5 km north of town. Painted red and grey, it's attractively decorated. Rooms give out on to an inviting grassy terrace overlooking the ocean and have very large beds, wooden floors, *esparto* blinds and a decent bathroom. The restaurant has an array of dishes from around the world including plenty of vegetarian options, and gives great ocean views. Breakfast is included.

€€€ **Hurricane Hotel**, Ctra N340 Km78, T956-684919, www.hotelhurricane.com. 6 km north of Tarifa, this beachside hotel is a deserved favourite, situated in a peaceful leafy garden. Although rooms are overpriced in summer, the hotel's facilities are excellent, including pool, internet, gym, beach bar, restaurant and pool table. There's also an attached kite and windsurfing school (see page 78), horse riding and bike hire. The more expensive (and better value) rooms face the beach. Breakfast is included. Book ahead.

€€€ **La Sacristía**, C San Donato 8, T956-681759, www.lasacristia.net. Pleasingly refurbished 17th-century building in the heart of town, ideal for a relaxing stay. There's a distinctly Japanese feel to the decor; rooms are simply but attractively furnished, with massive beds, tasteful lamps, floor mats, antique chairs and objets d'art, heating and fine bathrooms. The best one is an attic-like apartment under the dark wooden roof. Downstairs there's an enticing lounge with a fireplace. Some meals can be arranged (breakfast is included). Live guitar music some evenings.

€€€ **Room Tarifa**, C Silos 26, T956-682229, www.roomtarifa.com. Tucked into a great location in the old town, this boutique place offers small but beautiful rooms with modern bathroom facilities and an exceptionally cordial welcome. The roof terrace is the place to be for views over town in the early evening. A mite overpriced in summer perhaps, but that's Tarifa.

€€ **Casa Amarilla**, C Sancho IV El Bravo 9, T956-681993, www.lacasaamarilla.net. An excellent apartment-style hotel with refreshing art nouveau and North African interiors and light, comfortable and elegant rooms equipped with kitchen that offer very good value compared with other Tarifa options; it's slightly cheaper off season. Right in the heart of town. Recommended.

€€ **Hostal La Calzada**, C Justino Pertínez 7, T956-681492, www.hostallacalzada. com. Smuggled away up a side street near the church, this offers friendly folk at the front desk and very welcoming rooms, warmly decorated with a caring touch and featuring nice touches like ceramic vases and colourful tilework.

€€ **Hotel La Mirada**, C San Sebastián 41, T956-684427, www.hotel-lamirada.com. This hotel has cheerful rooms with nautically blue and white striped bedcovers, heating, TV and clean modern bathrooms. Pleasant and welcoming, it has breakfast available. It is a likeable option near the sea and excellent value in summer, so make sure you book well in advance at peak times.

€€ **Huerta Grande**, Pelayo s/n, T956-679700, www.huertagrande.com. A very peaceful complex of *casas rurales* set 15 mins' drive east of Tarifa in the Parque Natural de Los Alcornocales. There are wooden cabins and refurbished country houses, all well equipped and available as complete buildings or per room. The furniture is beautifully wooden and rustic; there are verandas for enjoying the sun, fine views, and a pool and restaurant.

€€ **Posada Vagamundos**, C San Francisco 18, T956-681513, www.posadavagamundos. com. This posh *hostal* has a fabulous location in the narrow streets at the heart of old Tarifa. Set in a well-restored old building, the rooms are unobtrusively stylish, if not particularly spacious. Noise can be a problem in summer. The café downstairs has a Zen feel and does pleasing mojitos.

€ **Hostal Africa**, C María Antonia Toledo 12, T956-680220, www.hostalafrica.com. This excellent budget choice is just inside the Puerta de Jerez on a quiet street in the old town. The rooms, with or without bath, are warmly welcoming, painted in attractive colours, and with seriously comfortable beds; there's also a roof terrace. The young owners are lively and welcoming; they can store boards or do washing. Recommended.

Camping

There are several campsites near Tarifa, strung out along Playa de los Lances.

Camping Tarifa, Ctra N340 Km 78, T956-684778, www.campingtarifa.es. Near the **Hurricane Hotel** by the beach and has good facilities including well-equipped wooden bungalows (€120) that fit a whole family. Open all year.

Río Jara, Ctra N340 Km 80, T956-680570, www.campingriojara.com. The closest to town at 4 km and a similarly relaxed spot. You can also hire horses here.

Algeciras *p70*
If you need to stay, there are numerous cheap options around the port, many of which are distinctly seedy.

€€€ Hotel Reina Cristina, Paseo de la Conferencia s/n, T956-602622, www.hoteles globales.com. A historic and elegant hotel set in gardens a few mins' walk from the centre. It's had many famous guests and was a hotbed of espionage during the Second World War. It's slightly faded now, but has excellent facilities including a pool and tennis courts. It gets quite busy in summer with package tourists; there's a minimum week's stay in Aug.

La Línea de la Concepción *p71*
€ Hostal Paris, C Sol 58, T956-171312, www.hostalparisenlalinea.com. Recently renovated, this friendly, and central place is sparklingly clean and has nondescript but comfortable rooms with bathroom. Private parking available.

℗ Restaurants

Conil de la Frontera and El Palmar *p65*
There are good seafood restaurants on the Paseo Marítimo. Heading up from here, the Plaza Santa Catalina has more bars and restaurants. C Hospital has many more tapas bars.

€€ Casa Francisco, Paseo Marítimo s/n, El Palmar, T956-232786. You can't miss this sturdy tavern in the hamlet of El Palmar; it's the main place to stay, have a coffee, or eat and does all in style. The restaurant specializes in fish baked in salt, which come out unbelievably succulent and juicy. All the seafood is of the highest quality and freshness, and prices are very reasonable.

€€ La Chanca, Paseo Marítimo s/n, El Palmar, T659-977420, www.casaslachanca. com. About 500 m south of **Casa Francisco**, this excellent place is a sort of ultimate *chiringuito* and one of the best spots in the zone for a drink. It's got a big garden with hessian parasols shading the tables, overlooking the sea. It's the perfect spot for a refreshing something while watching the sunset. It's also an upmarket place to eat, with delicious seafood rices, among other dishes.

€ El Gamba, Plaza Santa Catalina s/n, Conil, T956-440101. Right opposite the Torre de Guzmán is this ivy-covered bar and restaurant. It's popular for its terrace in the pretty square as much as for its high-quality swordfish and *mojama*, the cured tuna typical of the region.

Los Caños de Meca and Cabo Trafalgar *p66*
€€ Castillejos, Av de Trafalgar 10, T956 437 019. At the southern end of Los Caños, this attractively furnished courtyard restaurant blends a hippy-beachside vibe with some fairly ambitious plates and prices. They mostly succeed, with fresh fish, including red tuna, served with imaginative accompaniments. The upstairs terrace is a romantic place for a pre- or post-dinner drink.

€€ La Pequeña Lulu, T610-054979. At the southern end of the settlement, this café bar has an elevated position that means you're king of the castle as far as views are concerned. It's one of the places to be in the summer, serving bright and breezy plates of food all day, but shuts once the season's over.

€ El Mero, Ctra Zahora–Los Caños s/n, T956-437308. A *hostal* with a friendly restaurant. Excellent whole fresh fish cooked with plenty of crisped garlic costs only €10, and there's a cheap *menú del día*. It's on the main road 3 km north of Los Caños de Meca in the village of Zahora.

Barbate *p66*
€€€ El Campero, Av Constitución 7, T956-432300, www.restauranteelcampero. es. If you like tuna, this restaurant is reason enough to come to Barbate. It's all about that fish, and the various exquisite and tender cuts you can enjoy here take it to celestial heights. There's much Japanese influence in the preparation. The menu changes regularly, but such dishes as red tuna sashimi and tataki make toothsome appetizers before an exquisitely tender ventresca or fillet. Recommended.

€€ El Nani, Paseo Marítimo s/n, T956-453133. The best of the string of seafood eateries along the beach promenade. You can take away portions of fried fish, or sit on the terrace and enjoy the freshest seafood at knockdown prices; a big plate of mackerel (*caballas*) or grilled tuna, for example.

Vejer de la Frontera *p67*

€€€ La Vera Cruz, C Eduardo Shelly 1, T956-451683. This is a classy restaurant, set in a 16th-century chapel and enlivened by regular art exhibitions. There are creative and fine fish and seafood dishes such as *mero al whisky*, as well as excellent Retinto beef, wild boar paté and scrumptious desserts.

€€ El Jardín del Califa, Plaza de España 16, T956-447730, www.lacasadelcalifa.com. This amazingly atmospheric place is one of the best places to eat, reached via a series of stairs in **Casa del Califa** hotel (see page 72). There's a variety of intimate nooks to eat, as well as a garden and an open pavilion. The food is fantastic, with a North African/Lebanese bent. There are many vegetarian options and the prices are very reasonable.

€ Casa Rufino, outside town, in the village of La Muela, 2 km off the main road opposite Vejer, T956-448481. An excellent *venta* with Andalucían cooking. The dining area is very simply decorated, but the quality, quantity, and prices of things like mixed fried seafood, grilled king prawns, and steaks are exceptional. The *potajes* (stews) are also particularly good.

Zahara de los Atunes *p67*

In summer, you can't beat the *chiringuito* on the beach next to **Hotel Gran Sol**, which doles out tasty *raciones* of fried seafood to its busy terrace. Other eateries specialize in the wonderful fresh tuna.

€ Bar Paquiqui, C Pérez Galdós 4. This humble backstreet eatery has no pretensions but it's just about the best place in town to try tuna and other local seafood specialities like cuttlefish

croquettes. In summer, there's a covered terrace that's a great place for a leisurely lunch. Recommended.

Bolonia and Baelo Claudia *p68*

€€ Las Rejas, El Lentiscal s/n, T956-688546. One of Bolonia's smarter eating venues, this beachside restaurant specializes in *atún en manteca*, cold tuna in pork fat that's a famed delicacy of this coastline. They also demonstrate a sure hand with other fish dishes and warming stews.

Tarifa *p68*

There's a huge range of eating choice in Tarifa during summer, and places are constantly coming and going. In winter far fewer spots are open. Along Playa de los Lances, several of the hotels have excellent restaurants, while in town there are traditional Spanish options, several places offering different international cuisines, and various windsurfer spots with traveller-fusion cuisine and plenty of vegetarian choice.

€€ An 'Cá' Curro, C Moreno de Mora 5. T654-858012. A classy little establishment with a taurine theme, this tavern doles out superb *raciones* of high-quality produce. The pork dishes are succulent, the artichokes and the ham are also memorable. Recommended.

€€ Casa Juan Luis, C San Francisco 5, T956-684803. From the moment you enter this warmly welcoming backstreet spot through the kitchen – with succulent fresh produce on display – you know you're on to a winner. The menu focuses almost entirely on pork products, which are wonderful. Their bar opposite does *montaditos* and great *lomo en manteca*, pork cured in lard. Recommended.

€€ Mandrágora, C Independencia 3, T956-681291, www.mandragoratarifa.com. A romantic restaurant on a secluded street near the church, this is a Tarifa favourite. You can chow down on couscous or tagines, or stick to this side of the straits with Spanish seafood like octopus or sea anemones. There's plenty of vegetarian choice and a thoughtful selection of wines from around the country.

€€ Morilla, C Sancho IV El Bravo 2, T956-681757. This warm and busy restaurant is one of the town's best places to enjoy succulent fresh fish and typical cuisine from Cádiz province. The boss is friendly if a little pushy, but be sure to check prices before taking recommendations on the day's tastiest catch.

€€ Savarin Karpanta, C María Antonia Toledo 3, T956-682550. Open Easter-Aug. In the old town, this offers candlelit tables, polite service and a romantic atmosphere. The food delivers, with succulent, juicy tuna steaks the pick of the short but quality menu. Recommended.

€€ Souk, C Mar Tirreno 46, T956-627065, www.souk-tarifa.es. Thu-Sun 1000-1400 (breakfast) and 1900-late. An attractive and romantic basement restaurant charmingly decked out in North African style. The short menu is mainly Moroccan, although it adds several Thai and Indian curries. The atmosphere is great, the food average and the service friendly. Upstairs, the café serves delicious teas and snacks. Tough to find; it's 3 blocks back from the beach about 1 km from the centre.

€€ Vaca Loca, C Cervantes 6, T685-281791. Tucked away in the heart of old Tarifa, this bar is a popular evening destination. Though it can feel a bit touristy, what keep people coming are the outdoor tables, where sizzling offerings from the barbecue are served: huge steaks, sausages and brochettes.

€ Café Central, C Sancho IV El Bravo 10, T956-627025. A fine standby at any time of the day, this is Tarifa's most venerable café and a long-established meeting point in the heart of town. It has cold beer, a terrace, tempting tapas and well-priced fresh fish dishes.

€ El Francés, C Sancho IV El Bravo 21. This sweet little French-run tapas bar on the main street through the old town packs 'em in for its delicious, generous servings

of tuna and other delicacies. There's also a small side terrace for sit-down dining.

€ La Posada, C Guzmán 3A, T636-929449. This street has a few bars with a more local character than most in Tarifa, and this is one of the best. It's a small, committedly friendly place that offers a variety of *revueltos*, *montaditos*, brochettes and other goodies.

Algeciras *p70*

€ Las Duelas, C Alfonso XI 16. With a strong claim to the city's best tapas bar, this place is adorned with pictures of local bullfighter Fernando Ruíz Miguel in action (signed) and various Semana Santa Christs (not). They do fine smoked fish and a daily tapa special that is always delicious. It's just off Plaza Alta before the Ayuntamiento.

🎵 Bars and clubs

Vejer de la Frontera *p67*
Janis Joplin, C Marqués de Tamarón 6. Open 2130 to late, weekends only in winter. A well-known bar that attracts people from all over the region. The decoration is beautiful, a sumptuous neo-Moorish flight of fancy, and the music and company always reliably good.

Peña Cultural Flamenca, C Rosario 29. An atmospheric cavernous bar with weekend flamenco performances.

Zoco Flamenco, C Juan Relinque 28, is also a popular venue.

Tarifa *p68*
In summer action centres around the *chiringuitos* on the beaches and the latest ephemeral *discoteca*; off season the bars in the old town are quiet but the place to be.
Misiana, C Sancho IV El Bravo 18. This bar under the hotel of the same name is the most stylish spot in town, with designer lighting and chic furniture, including some very snug seating options. It's the most fashionable drinking option in town, but drinks are extremely expensive for Spain.

🔵 What to do

Tarifa *p68*
There are numerous activity companies, offering windsurfing, kitesurfing, climbing, biking, beach horseriding, quad-biking and whale watching among other things. The tourist office has a full list of operators.

Day trips to Morocco
Numerous agencies offer day trips to Morocco on the ferry; these include a guided visit to Tanger and lunch for around €60. There are more elaborate options with overnight stays, and trips to Fez and Marrakech.

Diving
Aventura Marina, Av Andalucía 1, T956-054626, www.aventuramarina.org.
Club Scorpora, Puerto Pesquero 15, T956-680576, www.buceoscorpora.com.
Yellow Sub, C Covadonga s/n, T956-680680, www.yellowsubtarifa.com.

Horse riding
Hotel Dos Mares, Ctra N340 Km 79.5, T626-480019, www.aventuraecuestre.com.
Hurricane Hotel, Ctra N340 Km 78, T956-689092.

Kitesurfing
Kitesurfing is big in Tarifa and there are 30 or more places to hire equipment or learn the basics, mostly along the main road. It costs around €90-120 for a 2-hr beginners' class. The best conditions depend on the wind, but are typically in the afternoon, so wait until morning before asking about conditions and booking your class.
Art of Kiting, C Batalla del Salado 47, T956-685204, www.artofsurfing.com, 2-day beginners' course €180.
Club Mistral, at Hurricane Hotel (see above).

Whale and dolphin watching
Several operators run whale- and dolphin-watching trips out of Tarifa: FIRMM, C Pedro Cortés 4, T956-627008, www.firmm.org, is the best, a marine foundation studying the area's cetaceans. They charge €30, run Mar-Oct, and trips should be booked a couple of days in advance. You are more or less guaranteed to see dolphins, and possibly pilot whales, depending on the season. FIRMM offer you another trip free if you don't see anything.

Windsurfing
Tarifa's 2 major winds, the easterly *levante* and the westerly *poniente*, create excellent windsurfing conditions along the beautiful Playa de los Lances, which stretches from town 11 km north. There are heaps of windsurfing schools that give lessons and hire equipment, including **Club Mistral**, at the Hurricane Hotel, Ctra N340 Km 78, T956-689098, and **BIC Sport Center**, at the Hotel Dos Mares, Ctra N340 Km 79.5, T630-342258. Board rental will cost about €50-60 per day, a full day's lesson is around €120.

🔵 Transport

Conil de la Frontera and El Palmar *p65*
There are 8-11 daily **Comes** buses from **Cádiz** to Conil, and some services from **Jerez**.

Los Caños de Meca and Cabo Trafalgar *p66*
Buses run between **Conil** and **Barbate** a couple of times a day; on Mon-Fri there are also 2 buses to and from **Cádiz**.

Vejer de la Frontera *p67*
There are 6 daily buses to Vejer from **Cádiz** (50 mins), and frequent buses to **Barbate**. For other destinations on the main road such as **Algeciras**, **Tarifa** or **Jerez**, you'll need to descend to La Barca de Vejer, on the N340 below town.

Zahara de los Atunes *p67*
There are 2-3 daily buses from **Cádiz** to Zahara run by **Comes**.

Bolonia and Baelo Claudia *p68*

In summer, buses run to Bolonia from **Tarifa**, but otherwise it's a 7-km walk from the main road or 1 hr's walk around the coast from Zahara de los Atunes.

Tarifa *p68*
Boat

There are 4 daily departures to **Tanger**, taking 35 mins. The 1-way fare is currently around €35; if planning a day trip, ask in a travel agents, who throw in lunch and a city tour for the same price as a return ticket. Anyone with a right to enter Morocco is allowed on (EU citizens, Moroccans, Australians, Americans, Canadians, New Zealanders and more). **FRS**, T956-681830, www.frs.es. Also offers car transport on their fast boats, and charge €37/93 per person/vehicle.

Bus

Comes buses serve Tarifa, and leave from Av Batalla del Salado near the Puerta de Jerez, T956-657555. There are 5 daily buses to **Cádiz** (1 hr 20 mins) 3 to **Jerez** and 4 to **Sevilla**. In an easterly direction, there are 10 buses to **Algeciras** (30 mins), falling to 7 on Sun, and 7 to **La Línea**, the entry point for visits to **Gibraltar**. 1 bus on weekdays travels to **Zahara de los Atunes**, **Barbate**, **Los Caños de Meca** and **Conil**. There are 2 buses to **Málaga**. In summer, buses run at weekends to **Bolonia**.

In summer, a local bus company, **Bus Tarifa**, T647-911691, runs a service from town along Playa de los Lances, stopping at hotels en route, and sometimes going as far as Bolonia. The schedule changes each year, so ring or ask at the tourist office for details.

Algeciras *p70*
Bus

Comes, near the train station on C San Bernardo, runs half-hourly buses all over the province. From Av Virgen del Carmen 17, opposite the ferry terminal, there are direct services to **Granada**, **Málaga**, and most other Andalucían capitals, as well as coast-hopping buses east along the **Costa del Sol**. There are also services to **Madrid** and **Barcelona**.

Ferry

C San Bernardo leads almost directly to the large modern ferry port, which is close to the town centre. Some buses arrive and depart from the ferry port itself.

There are several ferry companies operating services to **Ceuta** and **Tanger**. There are departures almost half-hourly to both destinations. The ferries take 2 hrs 30 mins, and cost around €40 1 way, and €75-110 for a car. Faster catamarans take 35 mins and are only marginally pricier. You can buy the tickets directly from the companies: **Euroferrys**, T956-651178, www. euroferrys.com; **FRS**, T956-681830, www. frs.es and **Trasmediterranea**, T956-583400, www.trasmediterranea.es, or from a travel agent in town or at the port.

Train

There are 3 daily trains to **Granada** (4 hrs), and 2 to **Madrid** (5 hrs). All go through **Ronda** (1 hr 45 mins) and **Bobadilla**, a junction where you can change for other Andalucían towns.

La Línea de la Concepción *p71*

As there's no cross-border transport, La Línea is where you get off for Gibraltar. The bus station is a block back from the frontier, and is frequently connected with **Algeciras** (half-hourly, 45 mins), **Málaga** via **Marbella** (4-6 a day, 2 hrs 30 mins), **Tarifa** and **Cádiz** (3-4 daily, 2 hrs 30 mins). There are also daily services to **Sevilla** and **Granada**.

❶ Directory

Tarifa *p68*

Language schools Escuela Hispalense, Av Fuerzas Armadas 1, T956-680927, www. hispalense.com, offers Spanish courses.

Gibraltar

The controversial British enclave of Gibraltar sits on a small headland completely dominated by its famous Rock, a spectacular mountain visible for many miles around. While one suspects that Britain would, these days, happily hand it over to Spain, the locals, who are for the most part a curious mix of Mediterranean races, staunchly demand that their opinion be considered, and an overwhelming majority of them, despite Spanish being their first language, prefer the status quo, with all the economic benefits of being a Vejer Casa del Califa tax haven and duty-free zone. There's now barely a British military presence here, but the settlement is busy with tourists, who come to see the monkeys and to buy cheap booze and fags, and sailors from docking warships. If you've just come from Britain, you probably won't see much need to visit, but if you crave a pint of bitter and a pub lunch, it's just the spot. It's well worth heading up to the Upper Rock for the spectacular views as well as the fascinating siege tunnels and the aggressive monkeys.

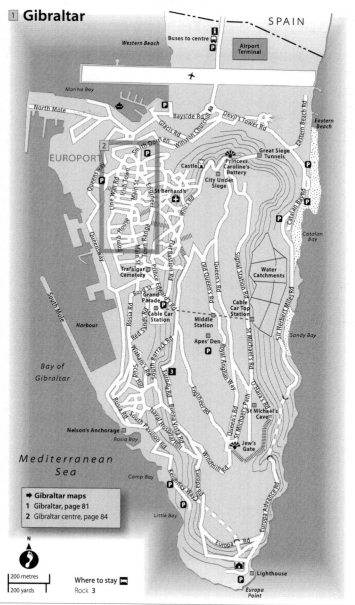

1 Gibraltar

SPAIN

Western Beach

Buses to centre

Airport Terminal

Marina Bay

North Mole

Bayside Rd

Glacis Rd

Winston Church

Devil's Tower Rd

Eastern Beach

EUROPORT

2

South Door Ln

Castle

Great Siege Tunnels

Princess Caroline's Battery

City Under Siege

St Bernard's

Queen's Way

The Wall Rd

Irish Town

Main St

Engineer Rd

Will Rd

Catalan Bay Rd

Catalan Bay

Queensway

Bomb House

Main St

Town Range

Bell Bastion Rd

Trafalgar Cemetery

Prince Edwards Rd

Boyd St

South Mole

Grand Parade

Cable Car Station

Water Catchments

Old Queen's Rd

Queen's Rd

Cable Car Top Station

Sir Herbert Miles Rd

Harbour

Red Sands Rd

Witham's Rd

Scud Hill

Barrack Rd

Middle Station

Apes' Den

Sandy Bay

Bay of Gibraltar

Rosia Rd

Europa Rd

3

Engineer Rd

Buena Vista Rd

Royal Anglian Way

St Michael's Rd

Queen's Rd

St Michael's Cave

St Michael's Path

O'Hara's Rd

Nelson's Anchorage

Rosia Rd

South Pavilion Rd

Naval Hospital Hill

Rosia Bay

Jew's Gate

Mediterranean Sea

Windmill Rd

Camp Bay

Keightley Way

Europa Rd

Europa Adrance Rd

Little Bay

Europa Rd

Lighthouse

➔ Gibraltar maps
1 Gibraltar, page 81
2 Gibraltar centre, page 84

Europa Point

200 metres
200 yards

N

Where to stay
Rock 3

Arriving in Gibraltar → *Phone code: +350. Population: 29,31.*

Getting there and around There are several daily flights to Gibraltar from London and other British cities, including with budget operators **Monarch** and **Easyjet**. The airport is at the entrance to the colony; you intriguingly have to cross the runway to enter the town. The border with Spain is open 24 hours. There's usually a long queue of cars, so most leave their motor in La Línea and walk across. You'll need a passport to get in, but you don't necessarily need a British visa; citizens of the EU, Australia, New Zealand, Canada, US and South Africa are among those who can enter freely. Visit www.gibraltar.gov.uk for details. You can't use a trip to Gibraltar to renew your permitted stay in Spain, as British officials won't stamp your passport. If you've only got a single entry to Spain, check with Spanish officials before crossing. There's no cross-border transport between Spain and Gibraltar, so you have to get to La Línea and cross on foot or in your own vehicle. From the border to the centre is a 15-minute walk. Buses (line 10) run from the border post along the length of town, a ticket costs £1 or €1.50.

Cars drive on the right in Gibraltar, as in Spain. Petrol is marginally cheaper here. Parking is difficult, but there's often space in free car parks on Line Wall Road or Queens Way. The main town stretches in a long line on either side of the pedestrianized Main Street. At the entrance to town is the open Casemates Square, from where the appealing Landport Tunnel runs towards the airport: this was once the only access to the citadel town. The Rock looms over everything; there are two access roads to the upper levels, as well as a cable-car at the far end of town.

Gibraltar essentials There are several tourist information offices. The most useful is the office on **Casemates Square** ① *Casemates Square s/n, T2005 0762, Mon-Fri 0900-1730, Sat and Sun 1000-1500*, and the booth in the customs building as you enter Gibraltar. There's also a **head office** ① *Cathedral Square, T2007 4950, Mon-Fri 0900-1730, Sat and Sun 1000-1500, tourism@gibraltar.gi*. There's a **police station** at 120 Irish Town.

Electricity current is the same as the UK, 240V, with three-pronged sockets. Electrical adaptors for European plugs are easily purchased.

The official language is English, but Gibraltarians mostly speak Spanish among themselves.

Currencies in Gibraltar are the Gibraltar pound and the British pound, although euros are accepted everywhere. It's worth getting pounds if you're going to stay a while, as exchange rates for euros in shops are usually poor. The Gibraltar pound, although equivalent to the sterling, is difficult to use in most of Europe; Spanish banks won't take it, so convert unused pounds into euros before you leave. There are several ATMs.

The country code for Gibraltar is +350, followed by the local number. Dialling Spain from Gibraltar, you must add the +34 international code. Payphones don't take euro. Gibraltar has its own mobile network, Gibtel; if you are using a Spanish mobile phone, you may want to manually select your Spanish operator so as not to be charged roaming rates.

Background

The rock's defensibility and numerous caves made it a Millionaires' Row for prehistoric hominids. Indeed the finding of a fossilized female skull dated to some 60,000 years was the first evidence of Neanderthals ever brought to light: found in 1848, the cranium, dubbed Gibraltar Woman, currently lives in the British Museum. In later times the Phoenicians knew Gibraltar as Calpe and in Greek mythology it formed, along with Mount Ablya on the other side of the Straits, the twin Pillars of Hercules. The Phoenicians had a town called Carteia 3 km away at Gibraltar Bay, from where Julius Caesar left in AD 45 to defeat the Carthaginians at the Battle of Munda.

When the Moors crossed the Straits in AD 711 under Tarik, governor of Tanger, they named the rock after their leader; *Jebel Tarik* (the mountain of Tarik), which became Gibraltar. The settlement was founded in 1159 by the Almohads, who constructed defences, reservoirs and a mosque. Gibraltar stayed in Moorish hands until a surprise attack by the Spanish, led by Guzmán El Bueno in 1309, but in 25 years it was regained by the Moors under Sultan of Fez after a 4½-month siege.

The Moors were finally evicted from the Rock in 1462 by the Spanish led by the Duke of Medina Sidonia. The Spaniards, who added to the fortifications, were to stay for a further 240 years until the War of the Spanish Succession. Although Britain supported the Spanish against the French, Gibraltar was taken by a combined Anglo Dutch fleet in 1704 led by Admiral Rooke. The inhabitants were told that they had to support the British-preferred claimant to the Spanish throne, Archduke Charles of Austria, or leave the Rock. Many did leave and founded a settlement at nearby San Roque, expecting to return shortly. Britain, however, gained formal sovereignty over the Rock in the Treaty of Utrecht in 1713 and has remained there ever since, despite Spain's diplomatic and military attempts to regain it.

The most serious attempts came in 1779 when the arduous Great Siege was to last over 3½ years. At the start of the 1800s, Gibraltar's strategic position was fully utilized during the Napoleonic Wars. After Nelson's victory at nearby Cape Trafalgar, his flagship *HMS Victory* limped into Rosia Bay, with the Admiral's body pickled in a barrel of rum. Some crew members are buried at Trafalgar cemetery.

Gibraltar played an important strategic role in both World Wars, but particularly the Second, when Hitler formalized Operation Felix, a plan to invade the Rock with Spanish support that never materialized. During these times the Rock became honeycombed with passages, augmenting the existing caves, used for ammunition storage, making a formidable fortress guarding the western entrance to the Mediterranean. It was during the Second World War that Winston Churchill, on hearing the legend that if the Barbary apes left the Rock, then the British would too, insisted for propaganda reasons that their number should never fall below 35.

In the post-war period, Franco continued to try to persuade the British to give up the Rock, but in a number of referendums the Gibraltarians have always staunchly voted to remain British. Franco eventually closed the border in 1965, however, this only served to make the *llanitos* even more anti-Spanish.

After the death of Franco and the entry of Spain into the Common Market, the borders were re-opened in 1985. In recent years, since the departure of nearly all the British forces, Gibraltar has made attempts to create some economic independence by forming a sort of financial Isle of Man in the Mediterranean, with mixed results. A casual attitude to financial regulation, including steps to combat money laundering – many companies based here are outside supervision and include many banks and internet gambling set-ups – have infuriated Spain and aroused the ire of the EU. Some controls came into place in 2010. The long-serving Chief Minister, Peter Caruana, who was re-elected in 2007, was generally a positive force for change of this sort, having clamped down on smuggling activities and improved relations with Spain. In late 2011, after nearly 16 years as chief minister, Caruana was narrowly defeated at the polls by a Labour/Liberal coalition led by Fabian Picardo.

Gibraltar has held referendums (declared illegal by the British government) in which a massive majority of the population have affirmed their wish to remain under the British umbrella (votes to become part of Spain haven't even reached three figures). While the governments of Britain and Spain seem prepared to come to a mutually acceptable agreement over the Crown Colony, the small matter of the wishes of the inhabitants has frustrated their designs. Still, Spain seems more accepting of the situation, and the surrounding area has benefitted from a flow-on effect. Former Spanish Prime Minister Zapatero's willingness to include Gibraltarians in the debate was another encouraging sign.

Much of the Gibraltar now in evidence is on reclaimed land; Dutch polder experts have been brought in to extend the usable land of the colony; the new Europort area is one recent expansion. The sea originally reached the high walls of the old town.

Places in Gibraltar

The original entrance to the **Lower Town** old district is through Landport, a tunnel that emerges in Casemates Square. Various fortifications snake their way up the hill and from here the walls run to the southern end of town. All the land west of the walls, including the recent development of **Europort**, has been reclaimed during the 20th century; the sea used to lap at the fortifications.

The **Gibraltar Museum** ① *Bomb House Lane, Mon-Fri 1000-1800, Sat 1000-1400 (last admission 30 mins before), £2,* is interesting, covering archaeology and history of the Rock. There's a 15-minute film, as well as superbly preserved 14th-century Arab baths and old photos and prints showing the colony in various stages of development. There's also a replica of the Neanderthal skull of 'Gibraltar Woman'.

Just outside Southport, the gateway at the southern end of Main Street, is the **Trafalgar Cemetery**, where some of the graves are of British sailors who died in the nearby Battle of Trafalgar in 1805. Beyond here is **Nelson's Anchorage** ① *Rosia Rd, Mon-Sat 0930-1715 (1815 summer), £1, free with Upper Rock ticket,* where there's the massive 19th-century Hundred Ton Gun. It was here that the body of Nelson himself was brought ashore, allegedly stashed in a rum barrel to preserve it for burial.

② Gibraltar centre

➡ **Gibraltar maps**
1 Gibraltar, page 81
2 Gibraltar centre, page 84

Governor's Inn
Apartments **3**
O'Callaghan Eliott **4**

Restaurants ❼
Café Rojo **1**

Where to stay 🛏
Bristol **1**
Cannon **2**
Emile Youth Hostel **5**

Bars & clubs 🍸
Angry Friar **8**
Clipper **6**
Lord Nelson **7**

At the end of the promontory is **Europa Point**, which has a mosque and a lighthouse. From here, it's easy to see dolphins and it's also a good spot for birdwatching.

The **Upper Rock** ① *daily 0900-1815 (0930-1915 summer), £10 (5-12 year olds £5) for all the sights, £0.50 if you just want to wander around, cars £2 extra*, is a large area that has spectacular views across to Morocco over the Bahía de Algeciras. There are several sights; to see them all in a short time, you're best off taking the taxi tour, see page 87. Another option is to take the **cable car** ① *1000-1745 (0930-1945 summer), last ascent 1715 (1915) and last descent 1745 (1945), closed days of high wind (relatively frequent), £9 return, £4.50 children*, leaving the Grand Parade. With your return ticket, you can stop halfway up to visit the Apes' Den. You can also walk up the rock, either following Willi's Road up past the hospital, or the path off Flat Bastion Road. It takes around three hours to cover all the sights on foot.

At the southern end of the Upper Rock, there's a superb viewpoint known as the **Jew's Gate** that looks across to Morocco and Algeciras. A monument commemorates Gibraltar's founding as Mons Calpe by the Phoenicians and its status as one of the Pillars of Hercules, marking the *non plus ultra* (nothing beyond) of the known world. Ascending from here, note the metal rings attached to the stone; these were used to haul cannon up to the batteries on the rock.

St Michael's Cave is an attractive if over-embellished limestone cave complex that was once believed to be the gateway to Hades, understandably as it sat atop a rock at the end of the known world. Other legends included the belief that it went down to an underground tunnel that led to Africa, and that this is how the monkeys first came over. The stalactites are mostly dead, but it's still worth a visit, especially to see a fascinating cross-section of a huge stalagmite with growth rings like a tree. There's an auditorium inside, and music playing to heighten the atmosphere.

Gibraltar's Barbary apes are in fact macacque monkeys, thought to have been brought over by the Moors. The only wild monkeys in Europe, they have thrived here, and are now wholly accustomed to humankind, to the point where their brand of aggressive cheekiness is something of a problem. They frequently grab tourists' bags if they suspect there are any foodstuffs within, and sometimes bite if they encounter resistance. You can see them all over the Rock, but they tend to hang out at the **Apes' Den**, where they get fed and are encouraged to pose for photos. Be careful around them though. If travelling by cable car, you can get off at the middle station for the Apes' Den, which is north from St Michael's Cave, on the way towards the siege tunnels.

Princess Caroline's battery offers more excellent views over the north part of Gibraltar and across to La Línea. Up the hill from here are the **Great Siege Tunnels**, the most interesting part of the Upper Rock. These were carved out of the mountain in the Great Siege of the early 1780s to bring guns to bear on the Spanish and French forces. The whole Rock is riddled with similar tunnels. Below the lookout is the mediocre City Under Siege exhibition; the colony has had 14 sieges, and historical documents describe conditions better than do the waxwork soldiers around this ruined bunker.

Near here, the Moorish Castle, used as a prison until 2010, stands guard high above the only landward access to Gibraltar, while the Military Heritage Centre, set in a gun battery, commemorates British services and has a display of weaponry.

Gibraltar listings

For sleeping and eating price codes and other relevant information, see pages 11-15.

● Where to stay

Gibraltar *p80, maps p81 and p84*
Price codes for Gibraltar are the same as the rest of the book (converted into euros). Better budget options are in La Línea (see page 71) across the border.
€€€€ O'Callaghan Eliott Hotel, Governor's Pde, T2007 0500, www.ocallaghanhotels.com. Just off the main street but removed from the bustle, this business hotel boasts an impressive array of facilities and great vistas from most of the rooms, though the view from the rooftop bar-restaurant tops the lot. You can often get much cheaper rates on the hotel's own page or other accommodation-booking websites.
€€€€ The Rock Hotel, Europa Rd, T2007 3000, www.rockhotelgibraltar.com. On the slope of The Rock itself at the southern end, this iconic Gibraltar joint is still the best address in town. Rooms have wonderful views over the Algeciras bay, and many have balconies. Excellent facilities include a pool and bar with live music, but it doesn't come cheap.
€€€ Bristol Hotel, 10 Cathedral Sq, T2007 6800, www.bristolhotel.gi. Attractive old building in the heart of town, with welcoming service and a small pool and terrace. The rooms are standard, with minibar, a/c, heating, phone and satellite TV. It's worth paying the £6 extra to get an exterior room overlooking the bay. Free parking.
€€ Cannon Hotel, 9 Cannon Lane, T2005 1711, www.cannonhotel.gi. This cheapie is just off the main pedestrian drag. It's pretty basic, but reasonable value for pricey Gibraltar. The rooms come with or without bathroom; a pleasant little patio and a bar are the best features.
€ Emile Youth Hostel, Montagu Bastion, Line Wall Rd, T2005 1106, emilehostel@

yahoo.co.uk. Gibraltar's cheapest acceptable option, this hostel is gruffly friendly and conveniently located just above Casemates Sq. Dorm beds are £17; try to get one of the smaller rooms for more peace. Price includes simple breakfast; there are also some singles and doubles. Reception open 0830-1030, 1630-2200, but you get a front door key.

Apartments
Email the tourist office for a fuller list of rental apartments in Gibraltar.
Governor's Inn Apartments, 36 Governor's St, T2004 4227, gibc@gibnet.gi. These offer considerable value compared to the rest of Gibraltar. With a double bedroom and sofa beds, they can sleep up to 5, and have a decent kitchen and satellite TV. Apartments cost £65 per night; there's a minimum stay applied in busy periods.

● Restaurants

Gibraltar *p80, maps p81 and p84*
Gibraltar has many British-style pubs. There are some good restaurants, and many pubs serve traditional fare all day at reasonable prices. Get away from Casemates Square and the main street for the best options.
€€ Cafe Rojo, 54 Irish Town, T2005 1738. Excellent-value bistro fare served in a friendly, intimate atmosphere. There are tempting mains like tuna steak, a wide range of innovative salads and delicious pastas. Plenty of vegetarian options and super desserts. Worth booking as it often fills.

● Bars and clubs

Gibraltar *p80, maps p81 and p84*
The Angry Friar, 287 Main St, T2007 1570. A busy pub with an outdoor terrace. Fine pub meals and decent pints. Opposite the Governor's residence; you can watch the changing of the guard from the pub doorway.

Clipper Bar, 78 Irish Town, T2007 9791.
Lively bar with a predictable nautical decor
and cheerful bar staff. Several beers on tap
and good-value generous dishes.
Lord Nelson, 10 Casemates Sq, T2005 0009.
A trendy bar open later than most with live
music, often jazz, with a small cover charge.

O Shopping

Gibraltar *p80, maps p81 and p84*
The astoundingly cheap cigarettes and
alcohol attract thousands each day. The
drawback is that, as Gibraltar isn't part of the
European Economic Zone, you can only take
normal duty-free limits back into Spain (ie
200 cigarettes and 1 litre of spirits per adult).

O What to do

Gibraltar *p80, maps p81 and p84*
Dolphin watching
A number of companies offer dolphin-
watching trips. These include: **Dolphin
Safari**, T2007 1914, www.dolphin safari.gi,
Dolphin World, T5448 1000 (T677-278845
calling from Spain), www.gibraltarinfo.gi,
and **Dolphin Adventure**, T2005 0650, www.
dolphin.gi. The trips last about 2 hrs and
cost around £25. You should see plenty of
dolphins and occasionally whales.

Taxi tours
A handy option for seeing the sights of the
Upper Rock is taking a tour by minivan-taxi.

This takes you around all the locations up
the hill for £15 per person (plus the entry
fee to the reserve, an additional £10 each).
Tours require a minimum of 4 people but, if
you ask, you'll usually be put in with another
group fairly rapidly. This can be arranged at
any cab rank; the best is the one outside of
Southgate. Make sure the driver takes you
to the Great Siege Tunnels, as they'll often
try and dissuade you so they can get back
quicker. Tour lasts 1½ hrs, longer and shorter
tours are negotiable. Try for a discount when
things are quiet. The drivers usually are very
good sources of information.

O Transport

Gibraltar *p80, maps p81 and p84*
On leaving Gibraltar by road allow time
for delays at the border. **FRS**, T956-681830,
www.frs.es, run twice a week from Gibraltar
to **Tanger**, but departures are unreliable, and
you're basically better off going to **Algeciras**,
where there are dozens of daily departures.

O Directory

Gibraltar *p80, maps p81 and p84*
Medical services The main hospital,
St Bernard's, is at the top of the town
on Castle Rd, T2007 9700. For non-
emergencies, go to the **medical centre** on
Casemates Sq, T2007 7003. **Post** Gibraltar
has its own postage stamps. The **post office**
is at 104 Main St; they don't accept euros.

Contents

Footnotes

Basic Spanish for travellers

Learning Spanish is a useful part of the preparation for a trip to Spain and no volumes of dictionaries, phrase books or word lists will provide the same enjoyment as being able to communicate directly with the people of the country you are visiting. It is a good idea to make an effort to grasp the basics before you go. As you travel you will pick up more of the language and the more you know, the more you will benefit from your stay. Regional accents and usages vary, but the basic language is essentially the same everywhere.

Vowels

a	as in English *cat*
e	as in English *best*
i	as the ee in English *feet*
o	as in English *shop*
u	as the oo in English *food*
ai	as the i in English *ride*
ei	as ey in English *they*
oi	as oy in English *toy*

Consonants

Most consonants can be pronounced more or less as they are in English. The exceptions are:

g	before *e* or *i* is the same as *j*
h	is always silent (except in *ch* as in *chair*)
j	as the *ch* in Scottish *loch*
ll	as the *y* in *yellow*
ñ	as the *ni* in English *onion*
rr	trilled much more than in English
x	depending on its location, pronounced *x, s, sh* or *j*

Spanish words and phrases

Greetings, courtesies

hello	*hola*	thank you (very much)	*(muchas) gracias*
good morning	*buenos días*	I speak Spanish	*hablo español*
good afternoon/evening	*buenas tardes/ noches*	I don't speak Spanish	*no hablo español*
		do you speak English?	*¿habla inglés?*
goodbye	*adiós/chao*	I don't understand	*no entiendo/*
pleased to meet you	*mucho gusto*		*no comprendo*
how are you?	*¿cómo está? ¿cómo estás?*	please speak slowly	*hable despacio por favor*
I'm fine, thanks	*estoy muy bien, gracias*	I am very sorry	*lo siento mucho/ disculpe*
I'm called...	*me llamo ...*	what do you want?	*¿qué quiere? ¿qué quieres?*
what is your name?	*¿cómo se llama? ¿cómo te llamas?*	I want/would like	*quiero/quería*
yes/no	*sí/no*	I don't want it	*no lo quiero*
please	*por favor*	good/bad	*bueno/malo*

Basic questions and requests

have you got a room for two people?	*¿tiene una habitación para dos personas?*
how do I get to_?	*¿cómo llego a_?*
how much does it cost?	*¿cuánto vale? ¿cuánto es?*
is service included?	*¿está incluido el servicio?*
is tax included?	*¿están incluidos los impuestos?*
when does the bus leave (arrive)?	*¿a qué hora sale (llega) el autobús?*

when?	¿cuándo?		
where is_?	¿dónde está_?		
where can I buy tickets?	¿dónde puedo comprar boletos?		
where is the nearest gas station?	¿dónde está la gasolinera más cercana?		
why?	¿por qué?		

Basic words and phrases

bank	el banco	market	el mercado
bathroom/toilet	el baño	note/coin	el billete/la moneda
to be	ser, estar	police (policeman)	la policía (el policía)
bill	la cuenta	post office	el correo
cash	el efectivo	public telephone	el teléfono público
cheap	barato/a	shop	la tienda
credit card	la tarjeta de crédito	supermarket	el supermercado
exchange house	la casa de cambio	there is/are	hay
exchange rate	el tipo de cambio	there isn't/aren't	no hay
expensive	caro/a	ticket office	la taquilla
to go	ir	traveller's cheques	los cheques de viajero
to have	tener, haber		

Getting around

aeroplane	el avión	luggage	el equipaje
airport	el aeropuerto	motorway, freeway	el autopista/autovía
arrival/departure	la llegada/salida	north, south	el norte, el sur
avenue	la avenida	west, east	el oeste, el este
border	la frontera	oil	el aceite
bus station	la estación de autobuses	to park	aparcar
bus	el bus/el autobús/ el camión	passport	el pasaporte
		petrol/gasoline	la gasolina
corner	la esquina	puncture	el pinchazo
customs	la aduana	street	la calle
left/right	izquierda/derecha	that way	por allí
ticket	el billete	this way	por aquí
empty/full	vacío/lleno	tyre	el neumático
highway, main road	la carretera	waiting room	la sala de espera
insurance	el seguro	to walk	caminar/andar
insured person	el asegurado/ la asegurada		

Accommodation

air conditioning	el aire acondicionado	dining room	el comedor
all-inclusive	todo incluido	hotel	el hotel
bathroom, private	el baño privado	noisy	ruidoso
bed, double/single	la cama matrimonial/sencilla	pillow	la almohada
		restaurant	el restaurante
blankets	las mantas	room/bedroom	el cuarto/la habitación
to clean	limpiar	sheets	las sábanas

shower	*la ducha*	toilet paper	*el papel higiénico*
soap	*el jabón*	towels, clean/dirty	*las toallas limpias/sucias*
toilet	*el inodoro*	water, hot/cold	*el agua caliente/fría*

Health

aspirin	*la aspirina*	diarrhoea	*la diarrea*
blood	*la sangre*	doctor	*el médico*
chemist	*la farmacia*	fever/sweat	*la fiebre/el sudor*
condoms	*los preservativos,*	pain	*el dolor*
	los condones	head	*la cabeza*
contact lenses	*los lentes de contacto*	period/	*la regla/*
contraceptives	*los anticonceptivos*	sanitary towels	*las toallas femininas*
contraceptive pill	*la píldora anticonceptiva*	stomach	*el estómago*

Family

family	*la familia*	boyfriend/girlfriend	*el novio/la novia*
brother/sister	*el hermano/la hermana*	friend	*el amigo/la amiga*
daughter/son	*la hija/el hijo*	married	*casado/a*
father/mother	*el padre/la madre*	single/unmarried	*soltero/a*
husband/wife	*el esposo (marido)/*		
	la mujer		

Months, days and time

January	*enero*	July	*julio*
February	*febrero*	August	*agosto*
March	*marzo*	September	*septiembre*
April	*abril*	October	*octubre*
May	*mayo*	November	*noviembre*
June	*junio*	December	*diciembre*

Monday	*lunes*	Friday	*viernes*
Tuesday	*martes*	Saturday	*sábado*
Wednesday	*miércoles*	Sunday	*domingo*
Thursday	*jueves*		

at one o'clock	*a la una*	it's six twenty	*son las seis y veinte*
at half past two	*a las dos y media*	it's five to nine	*son las nueve menos*
at a quarter to three	*a las tres menos*		*cinco*
	cuarto	in ten minutes	*en diez minutos*
it's one o'clock	*es la una*	five hours	*cinco horas*
it's seven o'clock	*son las siete*	does it take long?	*¿tarda mucho?*

Numbers

one	*uno*	sixteen	*dieciséis*
two	*dos*	seventeen	*diecisiete*
three	*tres*	eighteen	*dieciocho*
four	*cuatro*	nineteen	*diecinueve*
five	*cinco*	twenty	*veinte*
six	*seis*	twenty-one	*veintiuno*
seven	*siete*	thirty	*treinta*
eight	*ocho*	forty	*cuarenta*
nine	*nueve*	fifty	*cincuenta*
ten	*diez*	sixty	*sesenta*
eleven	*once*	seventy	*setenta*
twelve	*doce*	eighty	*ochenta*
thirteen	*trece*	ninety	*noventa*
fourteen	*catorce*	hundred	*cien/ciento*
fifteen	*quince*	thousand	*mil*

Food

bakery	*la panadería*	pork	*el cerdo*
banana	*el plátano*	prawns	*los camarones*
beef	*la carne de res*	raw	*crudo*
bread	*el pan*	restaurant	*el restaurante*
breakfast	*el desayuno*	sandwich	*el bocadillo/*
chicken	*el pollo*		*el sandwich*
egg	*el huevo*	sausage	*la longaniza*
fish	*el pescado*		*el chorizo*
fried	*frito*	scrambled eggs	*los huevos revueltos*
hot, spicy	*picante*	seafood	*los mariscos*
ice cream	*el helado*	soup	*la sopa*
lime	*el limón*	squid	*los calamares*
lunch	*el almuerzo/la comida*	supper	*la cena*
meal	*la comida*	sweet	*dulce*
meat	*la carne*	vegetables	*los legumbres/*
orange	*la naranja*		*vegetales*
pepper	*el pimiento*	without meat	*sin carne*

Drink

beer	*la cerveza*	juice	*el jugo*
boiled	*hervido/a*	lemonade	*la limonada*
bottled	*en botella*	milk	*la leche*
coffee/white	*el café/con leche*	soft drink	*el refresco/la bebida*
cold	*frío*	sugar	*el azúcar*
cup	*la taza*	tea	*el té*
drink	*la bebida*	water/carbonated/	*el agua/mineral con*
glass	*el vaso*	still mineral	*gas/mineral sin gas*
hot	*caliente*	wine, red	*el vino tinto*
ice/without ice	*el hielo/sin hielo*	wine, white	*el vino blanco*

Index